PANAMANIAN
SPANISH
SPEAK LIKE A NATIVE!

¡AYÁ LA VIDA! ¡CHUUULETA! DAME UN BOTE

¡P'alante! Salió el fulo ¡QUÉ CHÉVERE! Eso es chicha de piña ¿QUÉ XOPÁ?

LEE JAMISON

Visit us at insiderspanish.com

To all our Panamanian friends who,
though far from their homeland,
keep making sure of the more important things.

ACKNOWLEDGEMENTS

A WORK of this sort can never be accomplished without the help of many contributors. Foremost of all, I thank my wife Moraima for her continued encouragement and suggestions. Thanks as well to Marco and Alicia Casillas, Jason and Emily Provchy, and Consuelo Villegas for the office space provided during the preparation of this volume.

Much gratitude goes also to Eric and Argelis Chanis, Juan and Ileana Atencio, Epifanio and Nubia Atencio, Josué and Carol Delgado, Victor and Janet Kaa, Hans and Dayska Acevedo—all native speakers—for clearing up details about some of Panama's traditional sayings.

We are indebted as well to the local scholars who laid the foundation for the study of Panamanian Spanish. In the late 1950s Luisita Aguilar Patiño published her work entitled *El panameño visto a través de su lenguaje.* Her exhaustive 415-page volume ran the gamut from local flora and fauna all the way to customs of the farming community.

Then, in 1968, Baltasar Isaza Calderón and Ricardo J. Alfaro published *Panameñismos,* which earned the patronage of the Academia Panameña de la Lengua. More recently, in 2010, Margarita Vásquez published her *Diccionario del español en Panamá.* Filled with examples from the local press, the volume is the latest authority on Panamanian Spanish.

And, lastly, I am indebted to the people of Panama for their painstaking patience with all of us foreigners who have learned your most lyrical version of Spanish one explanation at a time.

insider*spanish*

Panama

TABLE OF CONTENTS

INTRODUCTION   9

SECTION 1 • A CONVERSATION PIECE   13

SECTION 2 • ALL IN THE FAMILY   37

SECTION 3 • A HARD DAY'S WORK   45

SECTION 4 • FOOD FOR THOUGHT   59

SECTION 5 • THE BODY HUMAN   77

SECTION 6 • ANIMAL KINGDOM   83

SECTION 7 • THE BRIGHT SIDE   93

SECTION 8 • THE DARK SIDE   109

SECTION 9 • A LITTLE PERSONALITY   141

SECTION 10 • THE GOLDEN ÑAPA   161

INDEX   163

INTRODUCTION

A MEXICAN was visiting Panama for the first time. The hostess at a family meal casually asked: **"¿Quiere que le dé chicha?"**. What the Mexican heard was: "Do you want me to *breast-feed* you?". But the real question was: Do you want something *to drink?*. **Chicha** is a generic term for any fruit drink.

In another conversation a Mexican suggested to his coworkers that they should depart for their destination **en bola.** He meant that they should go together. The Panamanians just giggled, because for them **en bola** means *naked*.

So the naked truth is that in the global community just knowing Spanish is not enough. Learning the country-specific peculiarities of the language is the only way to avoid costly misunderstandings. The goal of the *Insider Spanish* series of books is to help you to do just that. Imitating regional speech dignifies the locals. And even though to them you are the foreigner, some may well come to regard you as one of the family. Your efforts will definitely be rewarded—many times over!

Are you thinking of visiting Panama or are you living there now? Do you have family there or from there? Or are you just a language buff? Whatever the case, we urge you: Join the linguistic party! Instead of stubbornly clinging to phrase book Spanish, have an open mind! Embrace those new, but yet unfamiliar words and phrases! The more local words, phrases, and sayings you begin to use in your daily vocabulary, the more you will fit in.

One size does not fit all

The avalanche of books on Spanish has left us knee-deep in a language that no one actually speaks. Real Hispanics don't read out of phrase books. To them they are stale bread. Everyday speech is full of color that is country-specific. Consider:

The generic word for *white* is **blanco**. But when describing a light-skinned person, Mexicans will instinctively use the term **güero**. In El Salvador, Nicaragua and Honduras they say **chele**. Costa Ricans say **macho**. But in Panama it's **fulo**. (See term #18.)

That's where the *Insider Spanish* series comes in. In this volume, we don't teach you Spanish; we teach you to make your Spanish *more Panamanian*, to speak like a native. How? We have made an effort to identify 200 words and phrases that are endemic to the country. We cannot dogmatically state that they are only used in Panama. Immigration agents don't detain words at the border, as if they had need of passports. Nevertheless, *as a group* they are like a fingerprint that unequivocally identifies the Spanish of any given country. For any Panamanian who finds himself far from home, these words will be as captivating as the ringing bells of the ice cream salesmen.

Why 200?

One common saying is: **El que mucho abarca, poco aprieta**. It literally means: *He who tries to encompass a lot, squeezes a little.* The idea is that we shouldn't spread ourselves too thin. We give you 200 words and phrases because we want to satisfy your thirst—not drown you!

There is another consideration as well. My mother tongue is English and I have read many books on English words and sayings. And you know what? A large portion I have never heard in my lifetime! Never! Some Spanish language phrase books are just as all-inclusive. But how do you know if that phrase was known and used by 100 people or a 100,000? We save you the time by sorting that out for you. We hand you an eclectic selection to practice and perfect.

How to use this book

Panamanian Spanish: Speak like a Native! is divided into ten sections. Check out the table of contents and jump to the one that most interests you. Others read just one entry a day and then try to practice that new word or phrase as soon as possible. That way you *own* it.

Only one or two terms appear on each page. This will help your focus. For many entries a literal meaning is provided. This often sounds unnatural in English, but can be an aid to memory. Where the headings **In a nut-shell** appear, we help you understand the origin behind many of the popular sayings that make Panamanian Spanish such a delight to listen to. Sometimes we throw in a tip or two as to when using that phrase would be appropriate. Just a few pronunciations are provided for words that may initially throw foreigners for a loop.

In the main text, Panamanian words and phrases appear in **bold type**. Shortly thereafter the translation of the phrase will appear in *italics*. In many cases, sample sentences were ripped right from the headlines or newspaper articles that have appeared in the Panamanian press. *Insider Spanish* merely collects these quotes and they do not represent the opinion of the author. Since Spanish and English differ in punctuation styles, we here favor the English style even in Spanish quotes.

Lastly, feel free to use the terms listed here in everyday speech. Our selection is informal, but devoid of vulgarities.

Having understood this, dive in and enjoy!

1

A CONVERSATION PIECE

ALLÁ 'ONDE UNO

Literal meaning: there where one is from

In a nutshell: *Hecho en Panamá*, a local TV show, did a spoof on the country's rural residents. When these simple folk were asked where they were from, this was the answer. So if people are from **allá 'onde uno,** it means they are from the *boondocks*, or the *sticks*.

Following this same pattern, inhabitants of this region are also known as **interioranos,** literally *people from the interior.*

Residents of **allá 'onde uno** use more informal speech compared to their urban counterparts. To ask where you are going, they might say: **"¿Adónde vai tú?".**

¡AYA LA VIDA!

Literal meaning: Go life!

In a nutshell: This is one of the most common exclamations you will hear in Panama. It indicates surprise or consternation, depending on the context. While many spellings have been used, we have favored the above, because it is an abbreviation of **¡Vaya la vida!** Other variations include **¡Aya la peste!** , **¡Aya la máquina!** , and **¡Aya la bestia!** among several others.

BAJAREQUE

drizzle

In most Spanish countries **llovizna** is used. One local newspaper reported: "La falta de **bajareque** está afectando los cultivos de fresas en el distrito de Boquete." Translation: "The lack of *drizzle* is affecting the strawberry crop in Boquete District."

BIOMBO

a slingshot

On one occasion when Panama requested anti-drug resources from the US, a chief of police decried that "no le ha dado ni un **biombo** para enfrentar la situación." Translation: "He wasn't given so much as a *slingshot* to address the situation."

BOTE

Literal meaning: boat

Panama is inextricably connected to its world-famous canal. So it's no wonder that **Dame un bote** means: *Give me a ride*—all land vehicles included!

BUCO

(pronounced BOO-coh)

The French earn their spot in the portfolio of Panamanian Spanish with this entry, which means *a lot* in their vernacular. "Ese man está ganando **buco** dinero." Translation: "That guy is making *lots* of money." Other local synonyms include **pocotón**. (See also **rantan**, term #30.)

17

CHÉCHERES

In a nutshell: Do you have a lot of stuff? If so, you are well on your way to understanding the meaning of **chécheres!** It is the Panamanian catch-all word for *all your belongings.* When a renowned Latin actress recently split with her husband, the following headline appeared: "Thalía y su esposo empezaron la repartidera de **chécheres."** Translation: "Thalia and her husband have started divvying up their *stuff.*" Yikes!

CHÉVERE

In a nutshell: Panamanian Spanish has a definite Caribbean connection, and proof is seen with this term, well known in Puerto Rico, Cuba, and the Dominican Republic. **¡Qué chévere!** means: *How nice! How wonderful!* or *How cool!*, depending on the context. One listing of things to do had this heading: "Arranque súper **chévere."** Translation: "Super *cool* party." (See also **arranque**, term #112.)

18

CHEN CHEN

Literal meaning: money money

In a nutshell: Thousands of Chinese immigrants helped to build the Panama Canal. It's no wonder that Chinese elements have entered the local vocabulary. In Mandarin Chinese *chien* means *money*. In Panama the spelling was simplified and redoubled for emphasis. When some bus drivers threatened to strike, one headline declared: "Buseros del Oeste quieren su **chen chen.**"
Translation: "Western bus drivers want their *money*."

CAN YOU SPARE A CUARA?

What exactly is a **cuara?** It's the Panamanian way of saying a *quarter*, the 25-cent US coin. The 10-cent piece is a **daim**, that is, a *dime*. Panamanian coins still circulate together with their gringo counterparts. The main local coin is a **balboa,** but the principal currency is the US dollar.

CHIN

In a nutshell: Here is yet another loan from Chinese. It means a *little bit*. Panamanian singer Rubén Blades in his song *Te están buscando* spoke about some debt collectors that were looking to throw a bucket of cold water on top of a fellow who owed them money together with "un **chin** de electricidad," that is, a *little* electricity. Shocking!

Person A: ¿Cuánta bebida quieres?
Person B: Dáme solo un **chin.**

Translation:
A: How much do you want to drink?
B: Give me just *a little*.

CHOLO

In a nutshell: Those who speak Mexican Spanish may associate this term with Latin gang members in the United States. In Panama, though, **cholo** has a completely different meaning. Here it refers to *indigenous people* or *those with strong Indian features*.

It is also used figuratively to mean *dude*. "Oye, **cholo**, ¿cómo vas?" Translation: "Hey, *dude*, how's it going?"

A **cholipay** is an *attractive indigenous woman*. It's a combination of **cholo** and pie, as in the sweet apple variety. Someone with indigenous features can be described as **acholado**, and **pelo cholo** is *straight hair*.

HOORAY FOR CHOLYWOOD?

Move over Los Angeles! You are not the only filmmakers on the planet. Don't forget about the productions from **Cholywood**. What is that? A parodied name for the *Panamanian film industry*, a combination of **cholo** and Hollywood.

CHOMBA

In a nutshell: In racially diverse Panama **chomba** is the term given to *blacks.* And like most racial labels, **chomba** must be used with caution. For example, I am a white male who has lived in Latin America for parts of three decades. So I have heard the **gringo** label often. Does it offend me? Not necessarily. It all depends on who is saying it, how they say it, and in what tone. Use similar discretion in usage.

Even so, the Panamanian press uses the term unabashedly. When Mary J. Blige won nine Billboard Music Awards for work done on *The Breakthrough,* the newspaper *Día a Día* sported this headline: "La **chomba** arrasó." Translation: "The *black woman* took it all."

Chomba is not limited to skin color, but rather, can describe anything dark. A **lista chomba** refers to a *black list.* **Ají chombo** is *black pepper.*

¡CHULETA!

Literal meaning: Porkchop!

In a nutshell: Despite its literal meaning, this exclamation is 100% vegetarian! **¡Chuleta!** means: *Wow! Unbelievable! Incredible!* whether for good or bad. When it was discovered posthumously that the Cuban singer Celia Cruz had once performed secretly for Fidel Castro, a Panamanian daily wrote: **"¡Chuleta!** A estas alturas todavía no dejan descansar a Celia Cruz en paz." Translation: *"Unbelievable! At this late date Celia Cruz still can't rest in peace."*

PANAMANIAN PRONUNCIATION

To make your speech more authentic, lengthen the first vowel when you say: **¡Chuleta!.** Especially if you are really surprised, it will be more like **¡Chuuuuuuu-leta!.** Keep in mind that the locals pronounce **ch** like **sh,** especially in the middle of a word. For example, **muchacho** will sound more like **mushasho.** In words that end in **-ado,** the **d** is eliminated. **Pelado** is pronounced **pela'o,** and so forth. Listen and imitate!

COGER UN CINCO

Literal meaning: taking a five

In a nutshell: If in English someone tells you to take five, it means to take a break, presumably for five minutes. The Panamanians took this concept and made it better. For them **coger un cinco** means *to take a nap.*

On the other hand, **coger un cinco** isn't limited to a literal nap. One daily, talking about a singer, wrote: "El chico nos comentó que se está **tomando un cinco** para grabar su segundo CD." Translation: "The guy told us he's *taking a break* before recording his second CD."

COMER EN PAILA

Literal meaning: to eat from the pot

In a nutshell: A **paila** is a *pot*, of the cooking variety. But when members of a family excitedly talk among themselves, they might eat standing right in front of the stove. For this reason, **comer en paila** means *to talk a lot* or *to monopolize a conversation.*

In an opinion column, the Panamanian daily *Crítica* wrote: "Se escucha por allí que 'Tortugón,' tras la misa... cuando un periodista le hacía una pregunta incómoda, decía: 'Oiga, respete, estamos en un acto religioso,' pero cuando le tiraban una fácil, hablaba más que un narrador que **comió en paila.**"

Translation: "We hear that after mass when a reporter asked Tortugón [a parodied nickname for President Juan Carlos Varela] a difficult question, he said: 'Hey, show some respect, we are in a religious ceremony.' But later, when he was asked an easy one, he suddenly became like a narrator *talking his head off.*"

25

DIABLO ROJO

Literal meaning: red devil

In a nutshell: Take it easy. There's nothing Satanic here. This term refers to *public buses*. Originally US school buses, these units were imported, painted red, and given a new life. But their devilish reputation has to do with their *hired drivers*, known as **palancas**, whose recklessness is legendary. New, modern **metrobuses** are now taking over, and Greyhound-type units which travel between major cities are jokingly called **neveras**, literally *freezers*, because of their powerful air-conditioners. Now that's cool!

TURKEY ANYONE?

Public buses have onboard another worker in addition to the driver. That's the **pavo.** The turkey? Believe it or not, yes. He is the one who comes around and collects your fare, that is, he gobbles it right up.

26

CULISO

In a nutshell: The coolies were hired workers from China and India who originally came to Panama when the canal was built, and **culiso** has come from this label. Today in Panama it refers to *dark–skinned persons with straight hair.*

FULO

In a nutshell: Fulo is the opposite of **culiso,** and refers to *light skin color.* Luisita Aguilera Patiño in her book *El panameño visto a través de su lenguaje* traces the term to the Latin *fulvus,* which originally meant a reddish color. "El pela'o salió **fulito** como su papá." Translation: "The baby came out *white* like his father." **Salió el fulo** means: *The sun has come up.*

27

¡JO!

In a nutshell: Here's an abbreviation of the interjection **¡Carajo!,** which denotes impatience. If you preface a sentence with **¡Jo!,** you are telling your listener: Prepare to be impressed. When Jamaican track star Trecia Smith won the triple jump at the 2005 World Championship, the Panamanian caption read: **"¡Jooo chomba!"** Loose translation: *"You go girl!"* Notice once again that lengthening the syllable increases the amazement factor.

MAN

In a nutshell: This is another loan from English, only in the Panamanian version, it is unisex. "Ese **man** le dijo a esa **man** que se fuera." Translation: "That *guy* told that *girl* to leave."

MANSO

Literal meaning: meek

In a nutshell: This adjective is used locally as an intensifier. One headline read: **"Manso** tranque a Santiago."** Translation: *"Major* traffic jam heading to Santiago."* In an article about a Great Dane who won the Guinness record for the world's largest dog, the header was: **"Manso** perrón."** *"Huge* dog."*

¡METO!

In a nutshell: In the western province of Chiriquí, this is *Wow!* . When the local team recently won the baseball championship for the 13th time, the headline read: "13 veces, **¡Meto!**" Translation: "13 times, *Unbelievable!*" On the other hand, it can be used to express disgust. A parent may say to his child: "Te estoy hablando. **¡Meto!**" Translation: "I am talking to you. *Are you listening?*"

29

P'ALANTE

Literal meaning: ahead

In a nutshell: As we've seen, Panamanians prefer to economize syllables whenever possible. Why say **para adelante** if you can say **p'alante?** So, **dale p'alante,** means: *keep moving, keep going.* Ready to keep learning? **¡Dale p'alante!**

PIFIA

In a nutshell: When 475 lights first illuminated the Bridge of the Americas, the headline read: **¡Qué pifia!** Translation: *How elegant!* **Un carro de pifia** is *a luxury car.* "Karla está **pifiando** sus nuevos zapatos." Translation: "Karla is *showing off* her new shoes."

PILLAR

Literal meaning: to steal

In a nutshell: Pillar has three meanings depending on context. First, it can mean *to watch* or *to check out*. **"Pilla** este video." *"Check out* this video."

Secondly, it can mean *to take*. Just say **Pilla** while you are handing an item to someone. It's akin to saying: *"Here, take it."*

And, lastly, it can mean *to catch someone in a naughty act*. For example, one headline read: "20 menores **pilla'os** tomando licor." Translation: "20 minors *caught* drinking liquor." When you catch someone red-handed, it's enough to say: **"¡Te pillé."** Translation: *"Gotcha."*

31

PIQUETE

Literal meaning: a bite (as of an insect)

In a nutshell: Panamanians use it in the sense of *something sophisticated.* One man writing on heragtv.com described his fascination as a child with tiny packs of Nucita, a brand-name snack that was a small rectangle of spread made from chocolate, vanilla, and nuts. The package included miniature spoons. He says that the snack had a certain mystery to it. "¿Por qué había que tener tanto **piquete** para comérselo con su cucharita especial?" Translation: "Why was it so *sophisticated* that you had to eat it with a special spoon?"

If you buy something new, a friend might see it and say: **"¡Qué piquete!".** Translation: *"Aren't we high class?"*

A second usage of **piquete** is taken from the English *picket.* Notice this headline: "Manifestantes realizan en Panamá un **piquete** en apoyo a Zelaya y a su consulta popular." Translation: "Demonstrators in Panama *picket* in support of Zelaya and his popular referendum."

PONCHERA

Literal meaning: the punch bowl

In a nutshell: Ever been at a party where someone spiked the punch? If so, you can understand where **ponchera** got its start. These days **ponchera** can refer to *a wild party,* or some *cool or scandalous event.* "Borrachos formaron una **ponchera** en un metrobús." Translation: "Drunks *went wild* on the metrobus."

"De las **poncheras** más importantes que me rondan la cabeza está: 'Aceptar mi responsabilidad.'" Translation: "The most important of the *crazy ideas* floating around in my head is 'Accept my responsibility.'"

¿QUÉ E' LO QUE E'?

Literal meaning: What is what it is?

In a nutshell: This greeting translates as: *What's up?* or *What's new?*. Sometimes it's abbreviated even further. One columnist started his entry with "Epa, **queloqué!**". Translation: "*Hey, what's up?*"

¿QUÉ XOPÁ?

Pronounced KAY soh-PAH

In a nutshell: This is **¿Qué pasó?**, literally *What happened?*, with the final syllables transposed. If you run into a good friend you haven't seen in a long time, just say: **"¡Qué xopá, loco!"**. "*Hey, old man!*" Notice that **loco,** even though it means *crazy,* is here used as a term of endearment between good friends.

RANTAN

In a nutshell: This means *a lot of.* It is usually followed by the preposition **de.** "Tengo **rantan** de papel para reciclaje." Translation: "I have *lots* of recyclable paper." If you want to emphasize the quantity even more, use **tarrantan.** When twenty tons of drugs were found on a ship anchored in Panama, the headline read: "Decomisan **tarrantan** de droga." Translation: *"Tons* of drugs confiscated." (See also **buco,** term #6.)

TATÁI

In a nutshell: As adults, when we teach babies how to speak, we often use goofy terms that we think will be easier for them to pronounce. When Panamanian parents teach their infants to say goodbye, this is the term that is used. So for all your goodbyes, this is a more informal alternative to **adiós.** When a music producer retired, the press reported: "Dice **tatái** a la música." Translation: "Saying *farewell* to music."

DALE CUERO.

Literal meaning: Give it to the leather.

In a nutshell: While we usually relate leather to animal skin, it is used figuratively to refer to human skin in Spanish. **Cuero cabelludo,** literally *hairy leather,* is the everyday term for *scalp.* But when a Panamanian says, **Dale cuero,** he means: *Go for it!*

"Mi padre a veces me dice que no y luego a los cinco minutos, **dale cuero.**" Translation: "My father sometimes tells me no, and then five minutes later, he's like, *Go for it!*"

Dale cuero is a great shopping phrase. Once you've bargained a favorable price for an item, just let out a hearty: **Dale cuero.** It's like saying: *You got a deal!*

A similar phrase is: **Va el tiro.** "¿**Va el tiro** mañana?" Translation: *"Are we still on* for tomorrow?"

So are you now completely ready to learn Panamanian Spanish? **¡Dale cuero!**

2

ALL IN THE FAMILY

ABUELAZÓN

In a nutshell: For all of those grandparents out there who spoil your grandchildren, this one is for you. **Abuelazón** describes the exaggerated affection of grandparents towards their grandchildren. Do you let your grandkids decide where you will eat and when? Do you give them whatever they want, whenever they want it? If so, you are likely suffering from a case of **abuelazón.**

BUAY

(pronounced BWOI)

Here's another English loan by means of *boy*. It usually refers to a guy. "El **buay** cada vez que salía de su trabajo se iba a una conocida cantina." Translation: "Every time the *guy* went out, he went to a well-known pub."

CHANTIN

In a nutshell: This is likely from the English *shanty*, except in Panama it refers to any home, not necessarily one in poor condition. "Vamos pa' mi **chantin.**" Translation: "Let's go to my *house.*"

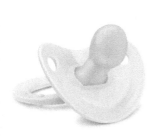

CHICHÍ

Literal meaning: baby baby

In a nutshell: In the Ngäbere language, **chi** is the word for *baby*. The Panamanians have doubled it for emphasis. When an actress refused to show her baby to the media, the headline read: "No mostrará a su **chichí.**" Translation: "She won't show her *baby.*" Take off the final accent, and **chichi** is a *girlfriend*.

CULECO

In a nutshell: Ever seen a hen brood over her newborn chicks? If so, you get the idea behind **culeco**. It describes the vicarious delight one encounters by experiencing life through one's offspring, or through other family members. "Marta anda bien **culeca** ahora que nació su sobrino." Translation: "Marta is really *excited* now that her nephew was born."

In Panama **los culecos** also refers to *an event during the Panamanian Carnaval* in which huge crowds listen to music and are sprayed down with water.

DARLE REJERA

To give a whipping

"A Roberto le dieron una **rejera** y más nunca jugó con fósforos." Translation: "They gave Roberto a *whipping* and he never again played with matches." Years ago parents told their children that the belt had a name and a purpose: **Martín Moreno, que quita lo malo y pone lo bueno.** So old "Mr. Moreno" took away the bad and put in the good! Now that's discipline!

39

GUIAL

(pronounced GHEE-ahl)

If there is a **buay**, there obviously has to be a **guial**—from the English *girl*. In everyday speech, it's used more for women. "Quiere conocer a la **guial** de la foto." Translation: "He wants to meet the *girl* in the picture."

INCHIPINCHI

In a nutshell: How close are you to your best friends? Are you so tight with them that you are only a figurative inch apart? If so, they are a true **inchipinchi,** or *close friend.* "Sandra es **inchipinchi** de Estela." Translation: "Sandra and Estela are *super close friends.*" (See also **pasiero,** term #124.)

QUITAFRÍO

Literal meaning: cold remover

In a nutshell: Wise Solomon wrote: "If two lie together, then they have heat: but how can one be warm alone?" That's the idea behind the **quitafrío,** the local word for *boyfriend* or *girlfriend.* Another similar term is **levante.**

PELA'ITO

Literal meaning: little Baldy

In a nutshell: How much hair did you have when you were born? Probably not much. So with good reason, *little kids* came to be known as **pela'itos,** the little Baldies. "¿Dónde dejaste a los **pela'itos?"** Translation: "Where did you leave the *kids?*"

THE DARLING RICE EATERS

Rice is a staple of Panamanian cuisine. It's no surprise, then, that **comearroz**, literally, a rice-eater, has become a local designation for *young children.* "¿Cuántos **comearroces** tienes?" "How many *kids* do you have?"

ZAMBITO

In a nutshell: In Panama's Azuero region, **zambitos** is used to refer to *small children between the ages of five and thirteen.* But in reality, the term is understood throughout the country. When Angelina Jolie and Brad Pritt were considering adoption some years ago, one local daily asked: "¿Adoptarán otro **zambito?**". Translation: "Will they adopt another *child?*"

3

A HARD
DAY'S WORK

AGARRAR LOS MANGOS BAJITOS

Literal meaning: grab the low mangos

In a nutshell: When I used to play basketball, there was a type of player we called the cherry picker. He never ran the court and never played defense. He just stood under the basket waiting for someone to throw it to him for an easy score. **Agarrar los mangos bajitos** is for the *cherry picker* in each of us. It means *to follow the path of least resistance* or *take the easy road.*

BIENCUIDA'O

Literal meaning: well-cared for

This refers to *informal parking attendants.* They will watch your car in a public parking area in exchange for a tip.

BOTELLA

Literal meaning: a bottle

In a nutshell: Say *bottle* and what comes to mind? I envision an empty bottle. If it had something in it, we would refer to its contents, for example a *bottle of beer*. But an empty bottle has little purpose. It takes up space, but does nothing. For that reason in Panama a **botella** is *someone with a cushy government job who works as little as possible*. And you can bet he's picking his mangos down really low! (Don't understand? See term #44.)

THE UNWANTED PACKAGE

We are thrilled when packages come, but locally there is a kind of delivery you wish you never had to deal with. Much like **botella** above, a **bulto**, literally a *package*, refers once again to *someone who takes up space, but does nothing*. Ummmm, excuse me, I've gotta get to work...

BRAVOS DE BOSTON

In a nutshell: In 1914 the Boston Braves were the worst team in the league, but they went on a tear and ended up winning the pennant. So to this day in Panama—more than a century later—if someone is said to be the **Bravos de Boston**, it means they are *excellent in their field, top-notch.*

CAMARÓN

Literal meaning: shrimp

In a nutshell: Do you like shrimp? In Panama not only is it a culinary delight, it's an economic necessity. Here **camarón** refers to *an odd job.* When there was work to be done, English-speaking employers just told the locals to *come around.* And **camarón** was born.

CARTUCHO

Literal meaning: a cartridge

A **cartucho** in most Latin countries is something you put into your printer when the ink runs out. But in Panama, it's the common word for a *plastic bag*. "¿Me prestas un **cartucho** por favor?" Translation: "Could you lend me a *plastic bag* please?"

CHAPISTERO

In a nutshell: Spanish speakers who work with metals know that a **chapa** is a *sheet of metal*. So for the Panamanians it's logical to call *body shop workers* **chapisteros**, and the trade, **chapistería**. But the rest of the Latin American world didn't get the memo. In other places, this work is known as **hojalatería** or **enderezado y pintura.**

CHINGUEAR

In a nutshell: If you learned Spanish in Mexico, you might be put off with **chinguear**. But, relax! There's nothing vulgar about it in Panama, although it's an activity that's not for everyone. It's the local verb for **gambling.** "Un lector me pregunta cuál es el diputado que se iba de viaje a Las Vegas a **chinguear.**" Translation: "A reader is asking me which congressman was going to go *gambling* in Las Vegas." So is it safe to use this word? You bet!

CLIPSADORA

In a nutshell: In most of Latin America the standard term for a *stapler* is **engrapadora**, because the staples are called **grapas.** But, not in Panama, where the de facto word is **clipsadora.** The verb is **clipsar,** *to staple.* To me it sounds like some Italian opera singer.
"Oh Clipsadora...be mine tonight..."

GUACHIMÁN

(pronounced wah-chee-MAHN)

In a nutshell: This term comes to us from the English *watchman* and has the same meaning. "Todas las escuelas deberían tener un **guachimán.**" Translation: "All schools should have a *watchman.*"

GUICHI GUAIPER

(pronounced WEE-chee WHY-per)

In a nutshell: When the torrential rains come, just flick these babies on, and voilà! Yes, these are *windshield wipers* said in perfect Panamanian Spanish. Really? Yes, *really.*

HIELO SECO

Literal meaning: dry ice

In a nutshell: Just say *dry ice* and your mind wanders...Your favorite rock star is about to burst onto the stage for one radical concert. Dry ice creates clouds of billowing smoke and spills into the audience. Special colored lighting sets an incredible mood, and then...and then...[back to Earth] you realize you are in a Panamanian classroom and someone asks for dry ice, or **hielo seco**, in the vernacular. Imagine your surprise when someone shows up with *sheets of styrofoam* used in arts and crafts projects!

Obviously at some point a local saw those sheets and he said what they looked like: solidified sheets of ice. And the name stuck. So the real question is: If your children use **hielo seco**, can they get brain freeze?

HUESEAR

Literal meaning: to bone

In a nutshell: What is Rover's favorite pastime? To sit and gnaw on a juicy bone for hours—not exactly a productive undertaking. That's why locally **huesear** means *to be lazy.* "Ese man golpea a los obreros que quieren **huesear.**" Translation: "That guy beats up the workers that are *slacking off.*" (See also **agarrar los mangos bajitos,** term #44.)

MOLA

In a nutshell: The Gunas are one of Panama's ethnic groups and their women are known for their artistic appliqué work, which they sell in *rectangular or square panels* known as **molas.** A Guna women proudly displays one of her molas at the beginning of this chapter.

MONTA'O

Literal meaning: mounted

In a nutshell: Years ago, if you were mounted, you were on a horse, but in such a position, you were higher up than someone on foot. So, today, if you are **monta'o** you are in a *better economic position* than your contemporaries. "Ahora que Pablo consiguió su nuevo empleo, está bien **monta'o.**" Translation: "Now that Pablo got a new job, he is *well-off.*" Unfortunately, though, sometimes people get high in another sense, and **monta'o** also describes a person who is *stoned*, or *armed* with illegal weapons.

PIQUERA

In a nutshell: The local word for a *public bus depot*. One headline read: "Conflicto entre taxistas por ubicación de **piquera.**" Translation: "Taxi drivers in conflict over *bus depot* location."

60

PULPEAR

Literal meaning: to make like an octopus

In a nutshell: We say we don't have enough hours in the day, so we might as well add that we don't have enough arms and legs to get everything done. If you were an octopus, you wouldn't have that problem. In Panama, **pulpear**, literally *being an octopus*, means *to work extra odd jobs* or *to moonlight* to make a living. "Algunos tienen que **pulpear** en varios empleos para ganar mejor sueldo." Translation: "Some have to *do some moonlighting* to earn a better wage."

REVOSH

In a nutshell: This is the Panamanian version of the English *reverse.* "El man pisó el clotch para poner el pickup en **revosh.**" Translation: "The guy engaged the clutch and put the pickup in *reverse.*"

SALOMA

In a nutshell: *"I've been working on the railroad...all the live-long day..."* Imagine the poor chaps whose job was to build the United States' first transcontinental railroad. Can you fathom digging and laying new rails day after day? How did they keep their sanity? One way was by singing as they worked. Panamanian agricultural society essentially learned the same technique. For that reason farmers developed the **saloma**, a *local type of singing usually accompanied by shouts.* If you have ever heard a **saloma** before, it sounds like a duel of two hound dogs howling trying to outdo each other.

TONGO

In a nutshell: According to the Real Academia Española, a **tongo** is a game that has been fixed. Perhaps due to police corruption, some felt they were playing a game whose winner had already been decided. Whatever the case, **tongo** is the everyday word for *cop*. When a thief impersonated a police officer, the headline read: "Se viste de **tongo** para robar." Translation: "He dressed like a *cop* in order to steal."

PROBLEMS? JUST CALL THE SMURFS

If you call the **tongos**, they might show up in a **pitufo**, literally a *smurf*, which is a *small blue pickup or sedan*. A regular police cruiser is a **chota**. If someone mentions a **policía muerto**, that is, a dead policeman, don't worry! It's the native term for a *speed bump*.

TRANQUE

Literal meaning: roadblock

In a nutshell: When the traffic gets bad, it is as if everybody is faced with a figurative roadblock. That's why **tranque** means *traffic*. "Graba a su esposa dando a luz en pleno **tranque.**" Translation: "He filmed his wife giving birth right in the middle of *traffic.*"

ZURRARSE

Literal meaning: to slide

In a nutshell: If you visit a park in Panama, your children will want to get on the **zurra zurra**, which is a *sliding board*. On the other hand, as a verb it means *to work extremely hard*. "Uno **se zurra** trabajando y ni le pagan lo que se debe." Translation: "You *kill yourself working* and they don't even pay you a decent wage."

4

FOOD FOR THOUGHT

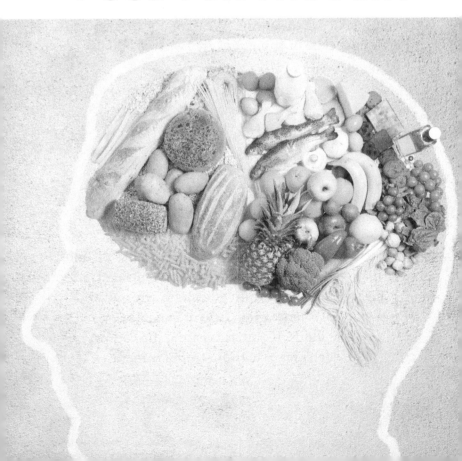

BURUNDANGA

In a nutshell: In Columbia **burundanga** is slang for *drugs*. But in Panama it alludes to something else you might be addicted to: *junk food*. "Salíamos para comer algún mango, caña o **burundanga** que habíamos comprado." Translation: "We went out to eat mango, sugar cane or some *junk food* we had bought."

CARIMAÑOLA

In a nutshell: Peel some yucca, boil it, mash it and fill it with ground pork or ground chicken, and cheese. Deep fry it until golden brown, and voilà —you have **carimañola**, one of Panama's prized, typical foods. If you are visiting the country, don't leave without trying some.

CARRIZO

Literal meaning: reed

In a nutshell: A reed is a tall, thin grass that grows in the wetlands. In Spanish a *reed* is **carrizo**, and the natives adopted it as the term for a *drinking straw*. "Pela'ito, toma este **carrizo** para tu bebida." Translation: "Boy, take this *straw* for your drink."

CHANGA

In a nutshell: If you are familiar with Mexican Spanish, relax! **Changa** is not a female monkey! Rather, here it refers to a *tortilla made from fresh corn*. "Quiero comer **changa** con queso blanco." Translation: "I want a tortilla made from fresh corn and white cheese."

CHICHA DE PIÑA

Literal meaning: pineapple drink

In a nutshell: A **chicha** is any *blended fruit drink*. But what if you are in a hurry and guests are coming? What's the easiest thing to do? Make **chicha de piña!** It's a no-brainer. Slice up some pineapple, throw it in the blender with some water and sugar. Pulverize, and bingo! You're ready. Because of the ease involved, if a Panamanian says, **Eso es chicha de piña**, it means: *It's a piece of cake.* A similar phrase, though not limited to Panama, is: **Es pan comido**.

EASIER THAN CHICHA DE PIÑA

The next time you are asked what you want to drink, just say, **chicha de policía**, literally *policeman's drink*. What is that? Just plain old *water*. Due to meager government budgets, the police have the reputation of having to make do with as little as possible. **Chicha de guardia** and **chicha de paipa** mean exactly the same.

71

CHICHEME

In a nutshell: Chicheme is a *milk-based drink*. It includes sweet corn or cornmeal with a smattering of cinnamon, vanilla and sweetened to taste. Delicious!

72

CHINGONGO

When the Panamanians saw for the first time *chewing gum,* pronouncing it in English proved far too difficult. And **chingongo** was born.

CHINO

Literal meaning: Chinese

In a nutshell: The Chinese initially came to the country to help with the construction of the Canal and then, the railroad. Being shrewd businessmen, though, soon they put up *small convenience stores* in local neighborhoods. Since most owners were Chinese, the stores themselves came to be known as **chinos.** "Vete al **chino** y cómprame chingongo." Translation: "Go to the *store* and buy me some chewing gum."

CHIRRISCO

In a nutshell: Where there's a will, there's a way. And if the people want liquor, known locally as **guaro** or **aguardiente,** they will make it if they have to. Meet **chirrisco,** Panama's version of *moonshine.* One headline read: "Desmantelan presunto laboratorio de **chirrisco.**" Translation: "Alleged *moonshine* lab dismantled."

CHIWIS

In a nutshell: Need a Band-Aid? Band-Aid is really a brand name for an *adhesive bandage*. But who asks for an adhesive bandage these days? Sometimes brand names become common nouns. And that's what happened to Cheez Whiz in Panama. It is a processed cheese product that was developed by Kraft Foods, but now it refers to *any snack*, regardless of the manufacturer. "Lo que el chino más se vende son los distintos tipos de **chiwis.**" Translation: "What the store mainly sells are different kinds of *snacks.*"

CONFLEI

In a nutshell: This is the Panamanian term for *corn flakes*. Locally, however, it is not limited in meaning to corn, but rather, refers to *any kind of cereal.*

CONCOLÓN

Literal meaning: with Columbus

In a nutshell: History tells us that Christopher Columbus landed in Almirante Bay in Panama on October 16, 1502. His last name in Spanish was Colón. Traditionally the captain ate last on the ship, so if you ate with Columbus, in Spanish you were eating **con Colón.** What is the staple food in Panama? Rice, of course. (See **comearroces,** in the box below term #42.) And when you get to the bottom of the pot, what is left? Burnt rice that stuck to the bottom. So to this day, that crunchy delicacy is known as **concolón.**

This idea is also used figuratively. If someone says, **Me metí a un concolón,** it means, *I ran into a lot of people,* or into *a lot of traffic.*

KICKING INTO THE RICE

In soccer, a *penalty kick* in Panama is known as a **tiro al concolón**, because at that moment players on the opposing team bunch up together, just like the bunch of rice on the bottom of the pot, but in this case to try to block the kick.

GUACHO

(pronounced WAH-show)

In a nutshell: Guacho is a *stew* loaded with yams, cassava, coriander, rice, vegetables, and usually some kind of meat—beef, pork tail, or pork skin.

Since a **guacho** is a mixture of many different ingredients, it can also be used figuratively. "Somos un auténtico **guacho** de virtudes y defectos." Translation: "We are an authentic *mixture* of virtues and defects."

According to the context, it can also denote *confusion*. "Vivimos en... un **guacho** politiquero, donde nada es verdad ni mentira." Translation: "We live in political *confusion*, where nothing is true or false."

BURN BABY, BURN

In most countries, if a newlywed wife burns the food, she might feel incompetent. But when it comes to **concolón**, she will be considered incompetent if she doesn't burn it. Burn baby, burn!

GUARAPO

In a nutshell: This is a *non-alcoholic drink made from sugar cane* and is used many in rural areas. Should the **guarapo** ferment, then it would be **guaro,** or *liquor.*

JORÓN

An attic space that is used either to store grain or as sleeping quarters.

It has the same emotional appeal for a Panamanian as when an English speaker hears the word "pantry." Locally there are several restaurants named "El Jorón."

MAFÁ

In a nutshell: Mafá is a braided snack made of fried flour. The product originated in Mahua, China, but Mahua in Chinese is pronounced **mafá,** and a snack was born. If someone tends to get himself in a mess, it might be said of him: **Es más enredado que un mafá.** Translation: "He's really gotten himself into a *mess.*" When lovers are making out, they may look like this twisted snack. "Ese man y su quitafrío están en un solo **mafá."** Translation: "That guy and his girlfriend are *really making out.*"

ÑAMPEA'O

Literal meaning: like a yam

In a nutshell: One staple that is greatly appreciated is the **ñame baboso,** which literally means the *slobbering yam*. It "slobbers" in the sense that when cut, it releases its natural juices. However, in Spanish **baboso** has another meaning. Since humans who slobber have usually lost their sanity, **baboso** can also mean *crazy* or *foolish*. This quality has semantically been passed along to the poor yam. So if someone is **ñampea'o,** it means he is *crazy,* either literally or figuratively. "Los vecinos decían que José había quedado **ñampea'o** desde la época de la dictadura." Translation: "The neighbors said that José had gone *crazy* since the time of the dictatorship."

We can also get a little crazy when we fall in love with someone. "El viejo estaba bien **ñampea'o** por la hija del soldado yanqui y se matrimonió con ella." Translation: "The old man was *head over heels in love* with the daughter of the American soldier and married her." Yams anyone?

MAMADERA

In a nutshell: In most Latin countries the generic word for a baby bottle is **biberón**. But Panamanian babies drink from their **mamaderas.** "Los bebés que siguen utilizando la **mamadera** más allá de los 12 o 15 meses de edad tienden a tener sobrepeso." Translation: "Babies that continue using a *bottle* after 12 or 15 months of age tend to be obese."

ENOUGH PEBRE FOR THE KIDS?

Everyone struggles to make ends meet—especially if you have a growing family. Putting enough food on the table can be a challenge. When broaching the subject, use the general word for food—**pebre.** "No sabía dónde conseguir una chamba para tener el chen chen necesario para darle el **pebre** a los comearroces." Translation: "I didn't know where to get a job so that I would have enough money for the kids' *food.*"

PATACONES

In a nutshell: Take green plantains, slice them, smash them, fry them, and voilà, you've got **patacones**—a delicious complement to any meal. On the Caribbean side of the country, these treats are known by the more generic **tostones. Hacer patacón** also refers to *throwing money in the air after a Catholic baptism.*

PEGA'O

Literal meaning: hit

In a nutshell: In this case you're hit by hunger. "Estoy **pega'o**." Translation: "I'm *starving*."

PELAR EL BOLLO

Literal meaning: to peel the bollo

In a nutshell: A **bollo** is a typical food similar to a tamale. It is a *mass of corn wrapped in a sugar cane leaf or a corn leaf.* When a loved one dies, it is a popular food to feed the mourners. For that reason, **pelar el bollo** is a euphemism for *death.* "Don Enrique **peló el bollo.**" Translation: "Don Enrique *kicked the bucket.*"

PINTA

Literal meaning: pint

In a nutshell: In Panama's steamy-hot tropical climate, there's nothing like a nice, cold **pinta**—the local word for *beer.* "Dame una **pinta.**" Translation: "Give me a *beer.*" Really large bottles of beer are known by the following terms: **mangalarga,** literally long-sleeve; **pescuezona,** big-necked; or **rompepecho,** the proverbial chest-breaker.

PIPA

In a nutshell: In many Spanish-speaking countries a **pipa** is a *water truck*, but in Panama it refers to a far more organic container: a *coconut*. On the other hand, if your friends start to refer to you as **pipón,** you're going to have to lay off the beer. **Pipón** means *pot–bellied*. You look like you have a coconut stuck inside your shirt! Oops!

PORCON

In a nutshell: Here's yet another loan from English. Enjoy all your movies with some fresh **porcon**, that is, *popcorn*. One classified ad read: "Se vende máquina de **porcon**." Translation: *"Popcorn machine for sale."* Another option is **millo**.

ROPA VIEJA

Literal meaning: old clothes

In a nutshell: Don't be alarmed! This isn't shredded thrift store attire. Rather, **ropa vieja** is *a typical dish made from shredded beef, onions, coriander, and tomato sauce.* It's usually served with rice, beans, and some fried plantains. But use moderation. If you eat too much, you might have to buy some new clothes!

SALTAR GARROCHA

Literal meaning: to pole jump

In a nutshell: Ever see the pole jump in the Olympics? It's amazing how the athletes are able to propel their bodies to incredible heights. Panamanians have taken this idea and applied it to their food regimen. Ever skip a meal? For locals it's more of a pole vault, and that's the idea behind this expression. "No todos pueden **saltar garrocha.** Ciertas personas deben abstenerse del ayuno." Translation: "Not everyone can *skip meals*. Some people should abstain from fasting."

SANCOCHO

In a nutshell: Sancocho is a tasty *chicken soup* loaded with onions, yams and **culantro**—a coriander herb similar to cilantro. Usually the chicken is a **gallina del patio,** or *free-range chicken.*

5

THE BODY HUMAN

93

COCOBOLO

Literal meaning: drunk coconut

In a nutshell: Are you follically challenged? Need a toupee? If so, locals will describe you as **cocobolo**, that is, *bald*. If you are in said condition, you will also be careful of vehicles that have a **quemacoco**, literally a head-burner. That's the native word for *sunroof!*

CHONTA

In a nutshell: Got a headache? Just say in good Panamanian Spanish: **Me duele la chonta.** Translation: *I have a headache.*

CHURRUSCO

In a nutshell: Got curly hair? If so, locally you will be described as **churrusco.** One young woman tweeted: "Prefiero andar con el pelo **churrusco** que ir al salón." Translation: "I prefer to walk around with *curly* hair instead of going to the beauty salon."

FARACHO

In a nutshell: Ever fainted after hearing bad news? If so, it will be said that you had a **faracho,** or *attack.* When a man entered into an epileptic fit, the headline read: "Le dio un **faracho** en el metrobús." Translation: "Man has an *attack* on the metrobus." The word is also used for heart attacks. Other similar terms include **beri beri** and **patatú.**

FIRI FIRI

In a nutshell: This colorful term means *wimpy, weak,* or *skinny.* Someone might say to you: "Eres un **firi firi.** No puedes cargar eso." Translation: "You're a *weakling.* You can't lift that." Of course, this can be used figuratively as well. *La Estrella de Panamá* reported: "Castañeda calificó como 'una propuesta **firi firi',** las modificaciones hechas al documento por los diputados de gobierno." Translation: "Castañeda described the modifications made to the document by the congressmen as a *'wimpy* proposal.'"

GOLPE DE ALA

Literal meaning: wing hit

In a nutshell: If you were a bird, your wings would be attached close to your armpit. So in Panama **golpe de ala** means *underarm or body odor*. It hits people right in the nose! "No hay nada peor que tener **golpe de ala.**" Translation: "There's nothing worse than **body odor.**"

This same stench can also be called **grajo,** and the adjective form is **grajiento.** "No hay excusa alguna para que alguien en este mundo esté **grajiento.**" Translation: "There's no excuse whatsoever for anyone on earth to *stink of body odor*."

THE MOST DISGUSTING SOUP

If you've ever played sports in a hot climate, you know what it means to be drenched in sweat. That pool of sweat—especially under the armpits—is jokingly called **sopa,** or *soup!* In basketball, a blocked shot is also called **sopa,** because sweat may fly in the act. One caption read: "Lebron James con **sopa** y 22 puntos." Translation: "Lebron James with a *block* and 22 points."

MOÑON

Literal meaning: big bow

In a nutshell: People with long hair often gather it into a pony tail. That gathered hair is called a **moño** in Spanish. So **moñon** is a big pony tail. If someone is said to be **moñon**, it means they have *long hair* and are sporting the hippie look. "Andas todo **moñon**. Debes ir a la peluquería." Translation: "Your hair is *really long*. You should go to the barber shop."

PECUECA

In a nutshell: Without proper foot care and especially in a humid climate, you might be unfortunate enough to suffer from **pecueca**. It's the *stench of stinky feet*. "Uhh, ¡qué **pecueca**! ¡Vuelve a ponerte los zapatos!" Translation: "Man, your *feet stink!* Put your shoes back on!"

6

ANIMAL KINGDOM

101

ERES COMO BORRIGUERO EN MOSAICO ENJABONADO.

Literal meaning: You're like
a lizard on soapy tile.

In a nutshell: Ever have so much to do that you started *running around like a chicken with its head cut off?* A **borriguero** is a *small lizard* which has problems on any tile floor—especially a soapy one. So if you are frenetically trying to get a job done without any real plan, someone might apply the above saying to you.

On the other hand, a **borriguero** is any *helper* on the job, probably because he has to spend a lot of time in the sun. "Se busca **borriguero** para albañil." Translation: "Wanted: bricklayer's *helper.*"

THE REPTILE RIP-OFF

When one container of pirated goods was confiscated, the headline read: **Vendían borriguero por iguana.** This literally means: *They were selling lizards as iguanas.* But the real meaning is: *They were getting ripped off!* How cold-blooded!

CAMINA COMO LORO EN CINC CALIENTE.

Literal meaning: He walks like a parakeet on a hot tin roof.

In a nutshell: When the sun comes out, the metal sheets used for roofing become extremely hot. Trying to walk on them would not be easy. So this analogy refers to *anyone who walks with difficulty.*

CHIVA

Literal meaning: goat

In a nutshell: Goats are independent creatures that tend to go anywhere they please. In Panama a **chiva** is a *small public passenger bus.* Larger, colored buses are **diablos rojos,** as we learned in term #16.

85

GALLO

Literal meaning: rooster

In a nutshell: The rooster has a great image in Latin America. In Nicaragua and Costa Rica the natives gobble up **gallo pinto,** a rice and bean dish. Throughout Central America there's a chain of appliance stores called **Gallo más Gallo.** The name means something like *The Valiant Rooster* and it sounds macho in Spanish.

But enter Panama and suddenly the poor rooster gets a bad rap. Imagine that a friend calls you one day to offer you a **celular gallo.** What's that? A rooster phone? No! Here **gallo** means *of poor quality, shoddy.*

DON'T BE CHICKEN!

Our poultry pals have other connections in Panamanian Spanish. A **gallada** is a *group of people.* "Allá va la **gallada.**" "There goes the *whole gang.*" On the other hand, if you attend a baseball game, you might sit in the **gallinero,** literally, the chicken coup. But it refers to *general seating.* If you sit there, you just might catch a *fowl* ball.

LO QUE 'TÁ PARA EL PERRO NO SE LO COME EL MICHO.

Literal meaning: What's for the dog, the cat doesn't eat.

In a nutshell: If something is meant to be, it is meant to be. That's the idea behind this saying. When a young man studied to become a disc jockey, he happened to run into someone who worked at a radio station and he ended up getting the job. This saying was applied to the way everything happened.

THE ASTUTE PANAMANIAN CAT

If you really want to sound Panamanian, then as you learned above, don't say **gato** for cat. Rather, use the local term, **micho**. A **micho** can also refer to an *astute man*. In fact, some men have earned the nickname **Micho.** Remember to pronounce it **misho.**

ME SIENTO COMO CUCARACHA EN BAILE DE GALLINAS.

Literal meaning: I feel like a cockroach at a hen dance.

In a nutshell: Ever feel out of place? Like you didn't belong? Like a fish out of water? In Panama, then you feel like a **cucaracha en baile de gallinas.**

"Mi amiga me invitó a su iglesia, pero creo que voy a estar **como cucaracha en baile de gallinas."** Translation: "My friend invited me to her church, but I think I would *feel really out of place.*"

MULA

Literal meaning: mule

In a nutshell: The mule is a beast of burden, resigned to carrying heavy loads. These days, however, in the commercial world the heavy loads are transported by large *semis* or *tractor trailer trucks*, known here as **mulas.** One headline read: **"Mula** cargada de azúcar se volcó." Translation: *"Tractor trailer* carrying sugar overturns."

OLD MCDONALD HAD A FARM...

When you hear Panamanians talking about local transportation, you might think it's a conversation about farm animals. Consider the following excerpt: "Una **mula** chocó con una **chiva** y se murió el **pavo**. El colmo es que para el pobrecito solo era un **camarón.**" Do you follow? Translation: "A *tractor trailer* crashed into a *small passenger bus* and the *assistant* died. The terrible thing is that for the poor guy, it was only a *temporary job.*" **E - I - E - I - O ....**

PAVEARSE

Literal meaning: to act like a turkey

In a nutshell: Turkeys like to strut their stuff. And students who skip classes do the same. So locally **pavearse** means *to play hooky.* "Un jovencito era buen estudiante, pero de la noche a la mañana comenzó a **pavearse** y a bajar las notas." Translation: "One young boy was a good student, but out of the blue he started *to play hooky* and his grades went down." A student who skips class frequently is a **paviolo.**

¡PONTE MOSCA!

Literal meaning: Make yourself a fly.

In a nutshell: Ever try to kill a fly with your bare hands? It's nearly impossible. Why? Because flies have amazing reflexes. So if someone tells you, **¡Ponte mosca!,** it means: *Be on your toes!* or *Stay alert!*

110

PERRO TINAQUERO

In a nutshell: At one time most trash cans in the country were made by Tin & Co., which stands for Tin & Company. But to a Spanish speaker, it looked like **tinaco.** That's why locals call *trash cans* **tinacos.** The neighborhood mutts would often scavenge for food in these cans. So to this day a **perro tinaquero** is a *stray dog* or a *mutt.* "Hay un **perro tinaquero** que el año pasado ocupó el primer lugar en la graduación de rescatistas caninos." Translation: "There is a *stray dog* that last year won first place in the canine rescue graduation." Some anglicize the word as **tainaker.**

SAPEAR

Literal meaning: to be a toad

In a nutshell: Toads are not the prettiest of creatures. And in the eyes of criminals, those who inform the authorities are no beauties. For that reason **sapear** means *to squeal.* What we equate in English with a rat or a weasel, Panamanians judge a toad. "Por cada tonelada de cocaína incautada, se cometen tres asesinatos: al que transporta, al que cuida y al que **sapea.**" Translation: "For every ton of cocaine that is confiscated, three murders are committed: the one who transports it, the one who takes care of it, and the one who *blows the whistle.*"

7

THE BRIGHT SIDE

ARRANQUE

Literal meaning: start

In a nutshell: In Spanish **motor de arranque** is the term for a *starter*, like the one in your car. But for Panamanians it is the start of something far more exciting: a party! "El gobierno se va de **arranque** la última semana de diciembre." Translation: "The government's going *to party* the last week in December."

BELLACO

Literal meaning: big and beautiful

In a nutshell: Are you fearless? Audacious and ready to take on the world? If so, then you are **bellaco!** The TV show *Hecho en Panamá* has a segment entitled "El más **bellaco."** Translation: "The most *fearless.*"

However, when used as a verb, **embellacarse** means *to become angry* or *irritated.* "Cuando no le dieron su pago el viernes, Yolanda **se embellacó."** Translation: "When she didn't get paid on Friday, Yolanda *got really upset.*"

CHANEADO

In a nutshell: This comes from the English word *shiny*. But in Panama it means *well-dressed*. Someone might say to you: "¡ Jo! 'Tás bien **chanea'o!**". Translation: "Wow! *You look great!*"

To compliment someone's dress, you can also say: "Estás bien **talla'o.**" This literally means: *You are really well-carved*. The idea is that the person is well-dressed —down to the most minute of details.

Yet another option is: "¡'Tás bien **rivetea'o!**". This literally means: *"You are well-riveted."* Ever admired the rivets on an old airplane? This phrase evokes the sophistication of that era.

CHOTEAR

In a nutshell: Imagine the scene: You're playing soccer and receive the ball. You make a move on your defender and go into turbo. With a quick strike you send the ball into the net! Your teammates converge on you with a series of high fives. That *act of effusive greeting* is described by the Panamanian verb **chotear**.

Of course, the greeting can be of a more formal variety. In one classified ad, a man offered a propane tank. He wrote: "Me puedes **chotear** por Whatsapp y cuadramos." Translation: "*Contact* me in Whatsapp and let's make a deal." **Chotear** can also be used figuratively. The Panamanian daily *Crítica* celebrated its 54th anniversary by writing: "Hemos **chotea'o** a este pueblo en sus momentos prittys." Translation: "We have *congratulated* this nation in its finest moments."

"Chotéame"
or
"¡Chotinnn!"

—HIGH FIVE

CHURUCA

In a nutshell: Take an elongated squash, perforate a hole in the side, and suck out the pulp. Then, with a knife delicately make vertical cuts on the side of the gourd. Finally, let the outside harden completely and cut off the stem. Now you've fashioned a primitive instrument; you've got yourself a **churuca!** To play this typical instrument, you take a **trinche,** *a two-pronged wire,* and strum the squash with it, just as a guitarist would use a pick to strum a guitar. Now you're making *organic* music!

"Los niños dejaron volar su imaginación e hicieron verdaderas obras de arte, cantaron y bailaron al ritmo de la guitarra y la **churuca."** Translation: "The children let their imagination run wild and created true works of art; they sang and danced to the rhythm of the guitar and the *squash instrument.*"

The person who plays the instrument
is a **churuquero.**

DONDE TOCA UNA LATA

Literal meaning: where they are playing a tin can

In a nutshell: Always ready to improvise, Panamanians won't refrain from playing a beat for a lack of musical instruments. Even a tin can will do. For that reason, **donde toca una lata** means *anywhere music is playing.*

ERES COMO CULEI.

Literal meaning: You are like Kool-Aid.

In a nutshell: Do you want to have a party but you're almost broke? No problem, mix together a little Kool-Aid and you are ready to go. Since this drink can be found at almost any festivity, if a local tells you: **Eres como culei,** it means you are a *social butterfly* and you never miss a party! I'll drink to that!

FREN

Literal meaning: friend

In a nutshell: This is yet another loan from English. "Yo te hablo claro, **fren.**" Translation: *"Friend,* I am being honest with you."

An alternative for friend is **compinche,** which is a *buddy.* One headline read: "Pistolero y el **compinche** quedaron arrestados." Translation: "Gunman and his *buddy* arrested."

Compa, an abbreviated form of **compadre**, is yet another local synonym. (See also **inchipinchi,** term #40, and **pasiero**, term #124.)

HACER UNA VACA

Literal meaning: to make a cow

In a nutshell: In English a cash cow is a business venture that allows you to milk the profits for years to come. In contrast, locally **hacer una vaca** means *to make a collection for a cause,* that is, *to crowdfund.* Speaking of one Little League baseball team with limited resources, a newspaper commented: "Para llegar al juego tienen que **hacer una vaca** para buscar un taxi." Translation: "To get to the game they have *to take up a collection.*" So if you need funds for a good cause, this might be your best moooooove!

A MONCHINCHE

In a nutshell: When you were a kid, did you ever grab hold of your father's neck for a *piggyback ride?* If so, you can relate to the sheer delight this term conjures up. "Papi, llévame **a monchinche.**" Translation: "Daddy, carry me *piggyback.*" Another variation is **a guanchinche.**

ÑAPA

In a nutshell: If you forget everything else you read here, don't forget this one! **Ñapa** could become your best friend and eventually cover the expense of this book. What is it? It is the local *baker's dozen.* So the next time you are at the market and make a sizeable purchase, just ask at the end: "¡Una **ñapita** por favor!". Translation: *"What will you throw in for free?"*

PARQUEAR

Literal meaning: to park

In a nutshell: Here's another term borrowed from English, but in the loan process the meaning changed. In Panama it is not just about parking your car, but partying! "Fui a **parquear** con mis amigos." Translation: "I went *partying* with my friends." It is also used as a noun, **parkin.** "Estos tres autores tienen un 'feeling' increíble entre sí a que después de un **parkin** llegaron a la conclusión de que había que hacer algo que rompiera esquemas." Translation: "These three writers felt such a powerful connection that after a *party* they came to the conclusion that they wanted to think outside the box."

THE SPECIALIZED PARKING LOT

Though **parkin** can also mean a parking lot, in Panama there is a special word for a public parking area that is exclusive to buses and taxis: **piquera.** One headline read: "Conflicto entre taxistas por ubicación de **piquera.**" Translation: "Taxi drivers in conflict over *parking location.*"

PASIERO

In a nutshell: In Portuguese, a *passeiro* is a passenger. And those passengers who traveled together frequently may have developed close friendships. That's the idea behind the Panamanian **pasiero.** One sportswriter posted this tweet: "Saints se despiden de TE Ben Watson y se traen a Coby Fleener **(pasiero** de Luck en los Colts/Stanford)." Translation: "Saints say goodbye to TE Ben Watson and bring Coby Fleener (Luck's *good friend* with the Colts/Standford)." (See also **fren,** term #119, and **inchipinchi,** term #40.)

PAY

In a nutshell: How about some apple pie? This term is pronounced the same as *pie* in English, but it talks of a different sweetie: a good-looking man or woman. When a Panamanian singer appeared at a concert with an attractive young woman, the headline read: "¿Será el **pay?**". Translation: "Could it be his *girlfriend?*"

PLENA

In a nutshell: Before reggae existed, in Panama there was **plena.** This is *Spanish-language reggae music.* "Aldo Ranks estrena en un pegajoso ritmo su nueva **plena.**" Translation: "Aldo Ranks debuts a catchy rhythm in his new *reggae song.*" On the other hand, imported foreign-language reggae is often referred to as **chombera.**

PRITI

In a nutshell: This comes from the English *pretty* and means essentially the same thing. "Es bueno tener ropa **priti,** pero no es lo más importante." Translation: "It is good to have *nice* clothes, but it isn't the most important thing." Try this: If you see something beautiful, just exclaim: **"¡Qué priti!".** Translation: *"How beautiful!"*

SARAO

In a nutshell: A **sarao** is a *school dance.* "Los estudiantes de la capital recibieron las vacaciones con un **sarao."** Translation: "Students from the capital marked the start of vacation with a *school dance."*

A CUALQUIERA SE LE MUERE UN TÍO.

Literal meaning: Anyone's uncle could die.

In a nutshell: If your uncle were to suddenly die, it wouldn't be your fault; it is a random event over which you have no control. That's why locally it means: *"It could happen to anybody."* The *Crítica* newspaper wrote: **"A cualquiera se le muere un tío,** y Justin Bieber no es la excepción, pues por segunda vez en dos años, el cantante se estrelló contra una pared de vidrio." Translation: *"Nobody's perfect,* and Justin Bieber is no exception. For the second time in two years the singer smacked right into a glass wall."

SARNA CON GUSTO NO PICA, Y SI PICA, NO MORTIFICA.

Literal meaning: Mange with pleasure doesn't itch, and if it itches, it doesn't mortify.

In a nutshell: Ever see a mangy dog? It is a pitiful sight. The miserable mutt scratches itself relentlessly, but to no avail. But what if in exchange for having mange, the dog could eat all the food it desired—juicy bones included? Would it take the deal?

That's the premise behind this saying that is used frequently throughout the country. One young Panamanian fell in love with a Mexican girl. He made plans to travel to Mexico and spend several weeks there. But before he bought the airline tickets, the girlfriend asked if he was really willing to make such a sacrifice to travel there. His answer: **Sarna con gusto no pica.** In other words, *It's worth it!*

TUNA

In a nutshell: There's nothing fishy about this local term. It refers mainly to a *traditional street dance.* "Con mucha alegría se realizó la tradicional **tuna** de tambores en la Villa de Los Santos." Translation: "With much fanfare the traditional street dance was celebrated to the beating of drums in Villa de los Santos."

To be honest, though, there is a little fishiness here. Even though the Spanish word for *tuna* is **atún,** many Panamanians have adopted the English form and use it instead. A recipe title read: "Dip de **tuna** para cualquier ocasión." Translation: *"Tuna* dip for any occasion."

THE PANAMANIAN MARIACHI

If you ever have opportunity to see a **tuna** in action, very likely it will be accompanied by a **murga,** Panama's answer to the mariachis. A **murga** is a *small musical group of wind and percussion instruments* usually present in local carnivals.

VIOLINISTA

Literal meaning: violinist

In a nutshell: If you are on a date with that special someone, what could be more romantic than a live violin performance? Of course, if the violinist never leaves your side, you might resent the lack of privacy. In Panama, a **violinista** is a *chaperone.* "Tuve la desgracia de servir de **violinista** para todas mis hermanas." Translation: "Unfortunately I ended up being the *chaperone* for all my sisters." I guess sometimes we just have to face the music!

8

THE DARK SIDE

A LA BULLA DE LOS COCOS

Literal meaning: To the noise of the coconuts

In a nutshell: Fancy a coconut? Do you think you can just stand under the tree and wait for one to fall? Of course not. No one knows exactly when coconuts will fall from above in a sudden barrage of thuds. It is simply unpredictable. For that reason, for locals **a la bulla de los cocos** means *haphazardly, without planning.* "Hay muchachos que estoy preparando y a los que están en la orquesta también, porque eso no es así **a la bulla de los cocos.**" Translation: "There are some guys I am training to be in the orchestra as well, so don't think it's just a matter of *hit and miss.*"

A LO MILI

In a nutshell: The military does what it wants, how it wants, and when it wants to.
So when a native does something
a lo mili it means *shamelessly, without regard for others.* "Maleantes lo usaron para robar **a lo mili."** Translation: "Some criminals used him to steal *shamelessly.*"

Another application could be: "William llegó al arranque **a lo mili."** Translation: "William showed up at the party *uninvited.*"

On the hand, if a Panamanian tells you, **Dale mili,** it means: *"Go away!"*.

111

ALBOROTAR EL CONGO

Literal meaning: to stir up the wasp's [nest]

In a nutshell: A **congo** is a type of *black wasp* whose sting is especially painful. Imagine the poor fool who takes a stick and hacks away at the nest! Soon hundreds of angry wasps will be in hot pursuit. For that reason, **alborotar el congo** means *to stir up trouble.* "Cuando el diputado llegó a la fiesta con su quitafrío, **se alborotó el congo.**" Translation: "When the congressman showed up at the party with his girlfriend, *it caused quite a ruckus.*"

DON'T BEE A FOOL

They say there's a sucker born every minute. But you don't have to be one of them! In Panama **congo** is also used to mean a *sucker*, a gullible person who is easily duped. So if someone says, **No seas congo,** it means: *"Don't be a sucker."*

ALCAHUETE

In a nutshell: In standard Spanish an **alcahuete** is someone who spoils others. Locally the meaning has changed slightly and is often used to mean *an accomplice.* One Brazilian drug lord quoted in a local newspaper claims: "No voy a actuar de **alcahuete** ni tampoco voy a delatar a nadie." Translation: "I am not going to be an *accomplice,* but at the same time I'm not going to snitch on anyone."

ARROZ CON MANGO

Literal meaning: rice with mango

In a nutshell: Hungry for some chicken and rice? Delicious! But what about rice and mango? Disgusting! It's a combination that doesn't work. Logically, then, **arroz con mango** means *confusion* or *chaos.* "Cuando dos chivas chocaron, se formó un tremendo **arroz con mango** ayer." Translation: "When two small buses collided yesterday, the scene became a *snarled mess.*"

ANDO ARRASTRANDO LA MANTA.

Literal meaning: I'm dragging my blanket.

In a nutshell: Remember Linus, Charlie Brown's friend? He and his blanket—his emotional crutch—were inseparable. When tired, we too may be dragging a symbolic blanket. So if someone asks how you are and your battery is low, just use this as your reply.

One sports headline read: "El Tauro FC continúa **arrastrando la manta.**" Translation: "The Tauro FC soccer team continues *sluggish.*"

An exhausted person might also sigh: **Estoy hecho añicos,** literally, *I'm in pieces.* It's akin to saying: *I'm totally exhausted.*

BABIECO

In a nutshell: Baba in Spanish is *saliva*. And if we start to lose it, we might drool. That's why here **babieco** means *foolish* or *stupid*. A poet sent a journalist a poem to publish, but the journalist forgot about it. Later he wrote: "Me lo dio el poeta Héctor Collado Mendieta para su madre, y yo de muy **babieco** no lo publiqué." Translation: "Poet Héctor Collado Mendieta gave it to me, but like a *dummy*, I forgot to publish it."

BARCO PARADO NO PAGA FLETE.

Literal meaning: A parked boat doesn't pay.

In a nutshell: Want to make money? Then keep your boats full and on the move. During a construction project, one woman complained about aggressive dump truck drivers. A politician responded: "Muchos ya han perdido los equipos ya que **barco parado no paga flete.**" Translation: "Many have lost their vehicles, because *a parked boat doesn't pay the bills.*" On this matter, we are all in the same boat.

BATERÍA

Literal meaning: battery

In a nutshell: Locally a **bate** is not just a baseball bat; it's also a slang term for a *lie*. "Estoy harto de tanto **bate.**" Translation: "I'm fed up with so many *lies*."

Another form of lying is cheating. For that reason, a *cheat sheet* is known as a **batería.** "Por debajo de su manga de camisa, tenía pegada una **batería.**" Translation: "He had a *cheat sheet* up his sleeve."

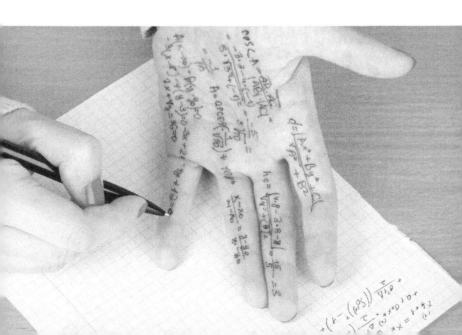

BOCHINCHE

In a nutshell: Want to hear the latest? Did you hear about...? If you feel compelled to be in the know about others, this word's for you! It means *gossip*. "El trabajo del fiscal es sobre evidencias de carácter objetivo y no sobre **bochinches** ni sobre conjeturas." Translation: "The district attorney's job is about objective evidence and not about *gossip* or conjecture."

I SAW IT ON BOCHINBOOK

These days many get their share of gossip through social media. So it's no surprise that some Panamanians humorously refer to *Facebook* as **Bochinbook.**

ME SALIÓ LA BRUJA.

Literal meaning: The witch appeared to me.

In a nutshell: Witches never bear good news. So this idiomatic expression means that something *went south,* or *went wrong.* One headline reported: **"Les salió la bruja** a ladrones de gasolinera." Translation: *"Everything went wrong* for gasoline station robbers."

"Parece que nos salió la bruja."

—I guess it's just not our day.

WHICH WITCH IS WHICH?

As the above example illustrates, **bruja** takes on different meanings in Panama depending on the context. If someone lives in a **barriada bruja,** he is in a *slum.* If he's in a **casa bruja,** it is a *shack.* In such circumstances, it is possible that the occupants are using **luz bruja,** that is, they are *illegally connected to the electrical grid.*

ESTAR EN BOSNIA

Literal meaning: to be in Bosnia

In a nutshell: During the early 90s a horrible genocide took place in Bosnia. Panamanians took the event and use it to mean *lost,* or *disoriented.* "Estos meteorólogos **andan en Bosnia.** Dijeron que habría sol y está cayendo un aguacero." Translation: "These weather forecasters are *out in left field.* They said it was going to be sunny and it's pouring down."

CACHARPA

an old jalopy

"Nos soplaron que su carrito es tremenda **cacharpa** y cuentan que echa más humo que una chimenea." Translation: "They let us know that his car is an *old clunker* and they say it smokes more than a chimney." This term can also be heard as **cacharpón,** the *big ol' jalopy.*

CAFÁ

a smack on the head

"Le dio un **cafá** para que prestara más atención a lo que hacía." Translation: "He *smacked him upside the head* so that he would pay more attention to what he was doing." Ouch!

ESTOY EN LA CAMA DE LOS PERROS.

Literal meaning: I'm in the dog's bed.

In a nutshell: If you get into trouble with your significant other, in English you are in the doghouse. But in Panama, if you are in the dog's bed, you have no money. If someone asks to borrow ten dollars, just answer with this saying. It means: "Look, man. *I'm totally broke.*"

Other ways to express the same idea are: **Estoy limpio; Estoy sin plata; Estoy pela'o;** and **No tengo ni un rial.**

120

CARILIMPIO

Literal meaning: clean-faced

In a nutshell: If good friends lie to you, it's easy to tell. You can read their faces. In contrast, crooks have so much experience hiding the truth that they keep a straight face. Only in Panama they keep a clean face. A **carilimpio,** then, is a *scoundrel,* a *bold-faced liar.*

"En cada contienda electoral viene otro **carilimpio** con un cuento nuevo y los engatuza otra vez." Translation: "In every election another *scoundrel* comes along with a new tale and fools them again."

CHIFEAR

In a nutshell: Have you ever waited for someone who never showed? If so, this is the verb for you. "Mirei **chifeó** ayer a los periodistas que pedían su opinión." Translation: "Mirei yesterday *avoided* the journalists who sought his opinion." So if someone doesn't show up, just ask: **¿Por qué me chifeaste?.**

CHIQUISHOW

In a nutshell: How do you feel when your children throw a temper tantrum in public? How embarrassing! Your **chiquillos,** or *children,* are putting on a show, but not one you are proud of. That's why in Panama a **chiquishow** is a *public scandal.* "Yolanda comenzó a gritarle a su marido en el mercado y le hizo el **chiquishow.**" Translation: "Yolanda started screaming at her husband in the market and *made quite a scene.*" Yikes! I'm getting out of here!

DESTAPAR UN TAMAL

Literal meaning: to uncover a tamale

In a nutshell: A **tamal** refers figuratively to a *problem.* Hence, if you uncover the **tamal,** you are exposing someone. **"Se destapa tamal** por tráfico de chinos." Translation: "Human trafficking of Chinese *exposed.*"

122

DE FIDANQUE A TOLEDANO

In a nutshell: Ever been forced into something you didn't want to do? This idea is expressed in the phrase **de huevo a huevo** in Spanish. Since locally there were two companies that sold eggs, Fidanque and Toledano, these company names were swapped in. **"De Fidanque a Toledano,** nos subieron el pasaje de los metrobuses." Translation: *"Against our will,* they raised the metrobus fare on us."

ES BUENO EL CULANTRO, PERO NO TANTO.

Literal meaning: The coriander is good, but not that good.

In a nutshell: Fresh **culantro**, a cousin of cilantro, is a tasty addition to a meal, but too much will ruin the dish. Therefore, this proverb means: *Don't overdo it.*

154

PURO TILÍN, TILÍN, Y NADA DE PALETA.

Literal meaning: It's just ring, ring, but no popsicles.

In a nutshell: As a child there's nothing more thrilling than hearing the ringing bell of the ice cream salesman who pushes his cart through your neighborhood. That distinctive tintinnabulation sends you running to buy your favorite treat. But imagine your chagrin when he tells you: "Sorry, but I'm all out." In a similar way, smoke blowers and sweet talkers excite us with their promises and then leave us out to dry.

"Las amenazas de paro en las rutas anunciadas para hoy quedaron en **puro tilín, tilín y nada de paleta.**" Translation: "It turns out that the bus drivers who threatened to strike were just *bluffing*."

ESTAR COMO GORGOJOS

Literal meaning: to be like weevils

In a nutshell: Weevils are small insects that eat seeds, which makes them a menace to granaries. But local superstition holds that there is a relationship between weevils and drought. "Los residentes en el distrito de San Félix denunciaron ayer lunes que actualmente viven **como gorgojos,** debido a la falta de agua." Translation: "The residents of San Félix district yesterday denounced that they are *living like weevils,* due to the lack of water."

Try this: If one day you don't have water at home, call up a neighbor and say: "Pasiero, échame una mano. Aquí **andamos como gorgojos.**" Translation: "Buddy, help me out. *We're as dry as a bone.*" The moral of the story is: The weevils, they wobble, but they don't fall down—not even for lack of water!

It's so dry in here.

You're tellin' me!

HASTA LA GUACHA

Literal meaning: up to the washer

In a nutshell: Ever fasten a nut and bolt? Especially if you are bolting wood together, you might slip a washer on before tightening. So from the nut's perspective, the washer goes right up against his head. Consequently, this local idiom means *up to maximum capacity, full.* "A través del ventanal veía que el sitio estaba **hasta la guacha** de gente." Translation: "I could see through the window that the place was **packed.**"

JUGUÉ MUERTO.

Literal meaning: I played dead.

In a nutshell: Ever taught your dog to play dead? It's a simple trick with no real purpose. As humans, however, we sometimes play dead in the sense that we are not alert to the opportunities or the dangers around us. That's the premise behind this local idiom. **"Jugué muerto** y me metiste gol." Translation: "I was *caught off guard* and you scored a goal on me."

There's a corresponding phrase that means the opposite: **jugar vivo.** One *La Prensa* reporter visited a fast food restaurant with limited seating. She writes: "Un pela'o me gruñó porque le **jugué vivo** con la mesa y me senté primero que él, pero ni modo: el tipo parpadeó." Translation: "A guy grunted in disapproval because I *beat* him to the table and sat down before him. Oh well, you snooze, you lose."

JUMA'O

In a nutshell: Had a few too many? Then you may have gotten a little **juma'o,** that is, *drunk.* "Él se bebió unos cuantos tragos, pero yo estaba más **juma'o."** Translation: "He had a few drinks, but I was even more *drunk."* Those who do get drunk will face the consequences the day after. That's when they will be **engoma'o**—with a *hangover.*

LORO VIEJO NO DA PATA.

Literal meaning: An old parrot doesn't stick his foot out.

In a nutshell: Can you teach an old dog new tricks? Most times the answer is no. This is the Panamanian version of the saying. When an old-timer failed to throw out the first pitch at a baseball game, it was commented: "Bien dice el refrán que **loro viejo no da la pata."** Translation: "Just as the saying goes: *You can't teach an old dog new tricks."*

MANGA POR HOMBRO

Literal meaning: sleeve in shoulder

In a nutshell: Have you ever noticed that when you take clothes out of the dryer, sometimes the shirt sleeves are pulled inside out—they're inside where the shoulder should be. That mental picture helps you to understand this idiom, which means *in a state of disorder.* "Los dos varones se pelearon, dejando todo **manga por hombro** y repartiendo huellas dactilares por toda la casa." Translation: "The two men fought, leaving everything a *mess* and leaving fingerprints all over the house."

MANZANILLO

In a nutshell: What do teacher's pets give their teachers? An apple, right? In Spanish *apple* is **manzana,** but to make words diminutive, the ending -**illo** can be added—**manzanillo,** the *little apple.*

So for locals **manzanillos** are *those who cultivate friendships for selfish interest.* They follow the rich and famous, seeking some benefit. When Justin Bieber appeared as a staff member for boxer Floyd Mayweather, the *Día a Día* newspaper asked in the headline: **"¿Manzanillo** de Mayweather?"**. Translation: "Is he Mayweather's *moocher?*"

MOCOCOA

In a nutshell: In Spanish **moco** is *snot*, and **cocoa** is the chocolate powder, just like in English. Panamanians use it to refer the *laziness or sleepiness that comes over us at certain hours of the day*. Depression can lead to similar symptoms. "Rosa Sofía estaba muy preocupada por su marido Juan, no sabía qué le pasaba, solo sabía que el man llevaba varios días con una **mococoa** muy grande." Translation: "Rosa Sofía was very worried about her husband Juan. She didn't know what was wrong with him; she only knew the man had been *very lethargic* for days." **Cabanga** is another local term for *depression*.

ÑÁÑARA

Pronounced YAHN-yah-rah

Fear. "Muchos ladrones acaban drogándose cuando les entra la **ñáñara** de caer presos." Translation: "Many thieves ended up taking drugs when the *dread* of getting incarcerated sets in." A **ñáñara** can also refer to *pimples* and *skin lesions*. Scared of that!

PATACONCITO

In a nutshell: Patacones are the delicious fried plantains we learned about in term #84. But **pataconcito** is something entirely different. There is a landfill which serves as the garbage dump for Panama City located at Cerro Patacón. When garbage begins to accumulate in other areas, people say it becomes a Little Patacón, or **pataconcito.** One headline lamented: "Poco a poco se forma un **pataconcito."** Translation: "Little by little a *small garbage dump* is forming."

PIEDRERO

In a nutshell: Piedra is *rock* in Spanish. But a **piedrero** doesn't work in a quarry. Rather, he snorts rock, that is, cocaine and other drugs. "Un **piedrero** fue detenido cuando hurtaba dos tanques de gas." Translation: "A *drug addict* was arrested after stealing two gas tanks."

PLOMO

Literal meaning: lead

In a nutshell: Years ago paint was tainted with poisonous lead. So lead became a problem. It still is in a figurative way in Panama. **Plomo** means either a *problem* or a *difficult person.*

One woman tweeted: "Para no decir algunas palabrotas, mejor decidí bloquearlo. Es un **plomo.**" Translation: "To avoid cursing, I just decided to block him. He's an *idiot.*" A young man posted this: "¡Que va! Esta rotonda en Multiplaza es un **plomo...** tranque, tranque." Translation: "How ridiculous! This Multiplaza traffic circle is such a *joke.* Nothing but traffic!"

On the other hand, bullets are also made of lead. So **darle plomo** can mean *to kill someone point-blank.* Many times this is used figuratively. "La gente estaba esperando las cámaras para **darle plomo.**" Translation: "People were waiting for the cameras to get there to start *criticizing him.*"

PONERSE EL CARRO DE SOMBRERO

Literal meaning: to put the car on its hat

In a nutshell: Where do you wear your hat? On your head. But in an accident in which your car overturns, the entire vehicle becomes a **sombrero,** or *hat.* "En Chiriquí el hijo de un diputado electo— en medio de la celebración—se enfuegó, **se puso un carro de sombrero** y mató a un perro." Translation: "In Chiriquí the son of a congressman-elect—right in the midst of the celebration—got drunk, *turned his car over,* and killed a dog."

PUSH

In a nutshell: Here's yet a another example of an English word used with an entirely different meaning. In Panama there are motels used for lovemaking in which the driver approaches in his vehicle, pushes a button, and enters a private garage. Once inside, there's a button with a sign that says PUSH. This button closes the door and he begins his illicit activity—all available at the push of a button. Of course, the method isn't foolproof. One man, stuck in traffic, started filming in front of one of these love nests. He tweeted: "Para que sepan, mientras grabábamos entraron más de cinco carros al **push.**" Translation: "Just so you know, while we were filming, more than five cars entered the *motel.*" Oops!

These hideaways are also known as **push button,** written in single form. "Construyen más **push button.**" Translation: "More *motels* being built." I think I'll stick to *push*-ups!

RADIO BEMBA

Literal meaning: big-lip radio

In a nutshell: Someone once quipped: "If you want to get the word out, use the three teles: *tele*-phone, *tele*-vision, and *tell a* woman." In Spanish, **bemba** refers to *big lips,* so **radio bemba** is a comical way to refer to *gossip.* (See also **bochinche,** term #42.)

"De verdad que **radio bemba** es más poderosa que Twitter, Facebook y que cualquier agencia de prensa internacional." Translation: "The truth is *word of mouth* is more powerful than Twitter, Facebook and any international press agency."

170

RAMBULERÍA

In a nutshell: Lack of respect is the order of the day, and **rambulería** takes it to new lows. It refers to *obnoxious speech and behavior*, especially when done to provoke others. After a paparazzo photographed Britney Spears without her permission, she threw a glass of water on him. The headline read: "Britney Spears le hace **rambulería** a fotógrafo." Translation: "Britney Spears gets *insolent* with photographer."

"Ni con gritos ni **rambulerías** se consiguen buenos frutos, hay otras maneras para vencer." Translation: "Screaming and *being rude* don't bear good fruitage; There are other ways to overcome [your frustrations]."

171

REPELÓN

a reprimand

"Toda la mañana viajé en el tren y no llegué a tiempo; por eso, mi jefe me dio mi tremendo **repelón.**" Translation: "All morning long I was traveling on the train, but I didn't get there on time. So my boss really *chewed me out.*"

ROSCA

In a nutshell: They say it's not about what you know, but who you know. Without connections, it would be difficult to get anything done. Locally, a **rosca** is a group with heavy influence—either for good or bad. "Para conseguir un trabajo en el gobierno hay que estar en la **rosca,** porque no los dan por méritos académicos." Translation: "To get a government job you have to have an *inside connection*, because they won't employ you based on academics alone." Another example: "Un sapo me dice que hay una **rosca** grande con los fuegos artificiales." Translation: "A snitch tells me that's there a lot of *favoritism* with the fireworks [contract]."

TRANSAR

In a nutshell: One headline read: "Banco **transó** un millón de dólares." Translation: "Bank *steals* a million dollars." In another context, a woman tweeted: "Vas a la máquina de chiwis o de soda, y te *transa* 0.10c porque 'tá daña'o." Translation: "You go to the snack or soda machine and it *rips you off* ten cents because it's broken."

RUNCHO

In a nutshell: Do you like to appear elegant? Then avoid everything that's **runcho.** "Ese suetercito sin mangas, y encima **runcho,** es un insulto a la elegancia." Translation: "That little sleeveless sweater is—above all—*passé;* it's an insult to elegance." What's never in style to be a cheapskate with your friends and family.

Notice another use of **runcho:** "No seas **runcho.** ¿Dónde están las sodas?" Translation: "Don't be such a *tightwad.* Where are the soft drinks?"

TENER LA BARRIGA PEGADA AL ESPINAZO

Literal meaning: to have your stomach pressed against a big needle

In a nutshell: *To be starving.* "Como el lugar abre a las 10 a.m., amén de que todos estábamos con el ombligo pegado al espinazo." Translation: "Since the place doesn't open until 10 a.m., we were definitely *starving.*"

ESTAR EN PANGA

Literal meaning: to be riding an old bicycle

In a nutshell: Remember the first bike you had as a kid? It was cool and in style—*back then!* But what if, as an adult, you hopped back on and rode around the neighborhood? People would view you as backward or old-fashioned. That's the basis for this colorful Panamanian phrase.

A: "¿Vas a la fiesta mañana?
B: "No."
A: **"Estás en panga."**

A: "Are you going to the party tomorrow?"
B: "No."
C: *"You are so boring!"*

So remember: If you fail to learn Panamanian Spanish, **¡estás en panga!**

insiderspanish

Panama

9

A LITTLE
PERSONALITY

ALELA'O

In a nutshell: Here's the local word for *crazy*, or *dumb*. "¿Tú eres así o sólo te estás haciendo el **alela'o?**" Translation: "Are you really like that or are you just pretending to be *dumb?*"

On the other hand, ever miss out on a good deal because you weren't paying attention? If so, in Panama that action can be described with the verb **alelarse.** "Había una oferta buenísma de boletos a Nueva York dos por uno, pero **me alelé** y no los compré a tiempo." Translation: "There was a two-for-one offer for tickets to New York, but *I blew it* and got there too late."

178

AMARRAR LA CARA

Literal meaning: to tie up one's face

In a nutshell: You are dying laughing and someone says: "Stop laughing. Be serious." Isn't it hard to suddenly change moods? Sometimes you wish you could instantly put your face into serious mode. Well, in Panama you can—at least figuratively. "El mandatario **amarró la cara** y exigió que lo respetara y luego ensayó una sonrisa." Translation: "The president *suddenly got serious* to demand respect and then cracked a smile."

ANDAR CON UNA PASTA

Literal meaning: to walk in pasta

In a nutshell: Ever seen the little machines that make pasta? The product comes out at a snail's pace. It is an adequate word picture for *slowness.* "Esperaba a mi abuelito hace una hora, pero como **anda con una pasta,** ¿quién sabe a qué hora llegaría?" Translation: "I expected my grandpa an hour ago, but since *he's as slow as molasses,* who knows when he will get here?"

ARREPINCHOSO

In a nutshell: Are you the life of the party? Then, this is your word! One man tweeted: "Realmente el panameño es **arrepinchoso.** No hay lluvia que lo detenga para cualquier evento." Translation: "Panamanians are such *party animals* that not even rain can keep them from showing up at an event."

181

BAGRE

In a nutshell: This literally means *catfish*—one of the least attractive creatures of the marine world. Locally it's used to refer to an *ugly woman*. One woman posted: "Jennifer Lawrence es tan bella; me hace sentir un *bagre*." Translation: "Jennifer Lawrence is so beautiful, she makes me feel like an *ogre*."

182

BICHARECO

In a nutshell: Who exactly is So and So? In Spanish the term **fulano** is used for this generic placeholder. But locally use this option. "Yo sabia que era el **bichareco** ese." Translation: "I knew it was *what's his name*."

BIRRIOSO

In a nutshell: Are you a fan? Do you lose track of time with your favorite hobby, with music, or maybe your sports team? Are you an unbalanced enthusiast? Then you will be dubbed a **birrioso.** A sportswriter tweeted: "¡Tremenda Serie Mundial! Yo **birrioso** desde chico." Translation: "Great World Series! I've been a *fan* since I was a kid."

"Nadie en la escuela era **birrioso** de estudio." Translation: "No one at school was *crazy* about studying."

146

CAMPECHANO

In a nutshell: Some people rub us the wrong way and with others we hit it off right away. **Campechanos** are the latter. They're the good guys. One woman posted: "Llegó Obama a la cena y dicen que comió sancocho al mediodía. Ohhhhh—un presi **campechano.**" Translation: "Obama came to the dinner and they say he ate sancocho [a typical soup] at noon. Wow! A *nice guy* pres.!"

GUAPACHOSO

In a nutshell: From the moment they enter the room those with charisma draw others like a magnet. Meet the **guapachoso,** the *lively, vivacious personality.* One girlfriend lamented: "Resulta que para la familia de mi novio debo de ser algo más **guapachosa.**" Translation: "It turns out that I wasn't *vivacious* enough for my boyfriend's family."

ESTAR EN BELÉN CON LOS PASTORES

Literal meaning: to be in Bethlehem with the shepherds

In a nutshell: When an angel appeared to shepherds to announce the birth of Jesus, they were likely engrossed in the message. Years later they may have reflected or even daydreamed about what they had seen. So if someone in Panama is said to be in Bethlehem with the shepherds, it means he is *distracted*. His mind is on a different planet.

A restaurant critic was visiting a certain eatery and was appalled at the substandard service she received from the waitress. What was the problem? "La chica simplemente **estaba en Belén con los pastores.**" Translation: "The girl was simply *out to lunch.*"

A man tweeted: "Les comparto el nuevo método para robar de los ladrones. Y los policías **en Belén con los pastores!**" Translation: "Here's a new method thieves are using to steal. And the police are *clueless.*"

A similar term is **estar en las nebulosas**—to have your head in the clouds. Mmm...I'm sorry. What were we talking about?

148

HABLAR EN CARRETILLA

Literal meaning: to speak with the wheelbarrow

In a nutshell: You are carrying a heavy load. Your wheelbarrow is filled to the hilt. And now you have to go downhill. Hope you have good brakes! With that word picture, you can only imagine that **hablar en carretilla** means *talking fast.* "No te entiendo. Estás **hablando en carretilla."** Translation: "I don't understand you. You're *talking too fast.*"

HACERSE EL CHIVO LOCO

Literal meaning: to make like a crazy goat

In a nutshell: Goats are aloof and happiest left alone. So if someone **se hace el chivo loco,** it means he is *ignoring* you. **"No te hagas el chivo loco,** que contigo estoy hablando." Translation: *"Don't give me the cold shoulder;* I'm talking to you."

MÁS PERDIDO QUE EL HIJO DE LINDBERGH

Literal meaning: more lost than Lindbergh's son

In a nutshell: On March 1, 1931 Charles Augustus Lindbergh, Jr., the son of the famous aviator, was abducted from the family home. Two months later the body was discovered and many considered the legal case that ensued one of the trials of the century. This idiom has forever burned the event in Panama's collective memory. It means to be *incompetent, clueless.* "El abogado ese que se presentó en debate abierto está **más perdido que el hijo de Lindbergh.**" Translation: "That stinkin' lawyer who showed up in open debate is *completely out in left field.*"

THE LOST CALL THAT ISN'T A LOST CAUSE

Cell phone calls used to be expensive, but Panamanians found a way to communicate on the cheap. If you want a friend to contact you, you call him, let it ring once, and hang up. It's a signal to get in contact. "Mándame una **perdida** a mi Whatapp." "Send me a *dropped call* on Whatsapp."

190

NO TENGO PEPITA EN LA LENGUA.

Literal meaning: I don't have any
fruit pits on my tongue.

In a nutshell: Imagine you're eating a juicy mango and
you have sucked the last ounce of juice out of the pit.
Just at that moment someone speaks to you. Can you
respond? It would be difficult. But if you didn't have
the pit in your mouth, nothing would keep you from
answering. So the phrase means: *I'm not shy about
speaking.* One girl posted this: "Lo siento, pero yo **no
tengo pepita en la lengua** con nadie." Translation: *"I'm
not one to mince words* with anyone." I don't know
about you, but I'm gettin' outta here!

PAGANINI

In a nutshell: Niccolò Paganini was an 18th-century Italian violinist. An urban legend has it that he befriended an 11-year-old virtuoso and gave him his violins and valuable manuscripts—an enormous gift! Despite the story's dubious authenticity, Panamanian Spanish celebrates Paganini with this proper noun. They use it to mean *the one who pays for everyone else.*

One woman tweeted: "Lo que hacen los funcionarios sin planificar, y luego el **paganini,** el pueblo como bobo." Translation: "Officials do things without any plan and then we the people, like dummies, are *left to foot the bill.*"

In a slightly different context, another woman wrote: "Jamás lograré entender de qué vale ser **paganini** en una relación." Translation: "I will never understand what's the point of being *the one who is always giving* in a relationship."

I guess there are always strings attached— just like Paganini's violin.

PICADO

Literal meaning: bitten

In a nutshell: Nobody wants to be bitten by a wild animal or an insect. But what if curiosity bites you? Will you come back for more? That's the slant Panamanians put on this adjective. "Quedé bien **picado,** yo quería ver la parte dos." Translation: "I *got hooked;* I wanted to see part two."

"Quedé **picado** por el tema de quién era peor dictador: Torrijos o Noriega." Translation: "I was intrigued by the subject of who was the worst dictator: Torrijos or Noriega."

PILINQUI

cheapskate

"Quien se lo dio era un **pilinqui,** porque el regalo no costaba mucho." Translation: "Whoever gave it to him was a real *tightwad,* because the gift didn't cost much." Other synonyms include **truñuño** and **pichicuma.**

RACATACA

In a nutshell: Criminal activity seems to go from bad to worse. Who are the perpetrators? Many would blame the **racataca**—a broad term that encompasses gang members, criminals, and those who embody the hip-hop lifestyle. It can also be an adjective meaning the *unrefined, uneducated,* or *poor.*

One writer for *Ellas* magazine spoke of an unpleasant experience she had at a theme park. A child was kicking the back of her chair and the kid's mother refused to make him stop. Indignant, she wrote: "No vale la pena coger mala sangre por culpa de una **racataca.**" Translation: "It's not worth harboring resentment on account of *someone with no class.*"

Use the term with caution, as some consider it derogatory. **Racataca** is the exact opposite of **yeyé.** (See **yeyé,** term #200.)

RAYARSE

Literal meaning: to scratch or cross out

In a nutshell: When we are angry, we may cross people off our list—cross them out. This verb conveys the same idea. **"¡Se rayó** Karen con la puntuación!" Translation: "Karen was *furious* when she saw her score!"

RUMBERO

In a nutshell: Locally a party is known as a **rumba.** So if you are a **rumbero,** you're a *partyer!* One man posted: "No soy **rumbero,** pero la soledad me obliga." Translation: "I'm not a *partyer,* but loneliness compels me." Another man wrote: "Algunas personas tienen un **rumbero** interior por descubrir." Translation: "Inside some of us there's a *party animal* waiting to get out."

NO DANCING PARTNER? JUST EAT TURKEY

Pity the poor girl who goes to the dance, but no one invites her onto the floor—not even once. What does she do? According to a local idiom, apparently she eats turkey. **Comer pavo** conveys precisely that idea. "Juanita se fue a la fiesta, pero solo quedó **comiendo pavo.**" Translation: "Juanita went to the party, but *no one invited her to dance.*" If she wanted to quit this habit, could she go cold turkey?

SALÍRSELE EL COBRE

Literal meaning: to have one's copper come out

In a nutshell: Squeeze an orange and you get orange juice. Squeeze wire hard enough and the copper comes out. This phrase, then, means *to show your true colors*, but usually for the worst. "No pueden mantener una conversación sin que **se les salga el cobre.**" Translation: "They can't hold a conversation without *losing their composure*."

SABE MÁS QUE TÍO CONEJO.

Literal meaning: He knows more than Uncle Rabbit.

In a nutshell: Tío Conejo, or Uncle Rabbit, is a fictional character who always outsmarted **tío Coyote,** Uncle Coyote. One man tweeted: "Bien transa'o está el florista este, queriendo **ser más vivo que tío Conejo.''** Translation: "This florist is a real shyster; he's got more tricks up his sleeve than Uncle Rabbit." Think of **tío Conejo** as Panama's version of Bugs Bunny.

VIDAJENA

Literal meaning: someone else's life

In a nutshell: Always sticking your nose in where it doesn't belong? If so, in Panama you'll be called a **vidajena.** "Si no fuéramos tan **vidajena,** no hubiera tranque." Translation: "If we weren't such *rubberneckers*, there wouldn't be a traffic jam." Another complained: "Ya casi me duermo y mi hermanita no me deja; **vidajena** mirando mis chats." Translation: "I'm almost ready to fall asleep and my little sister doesn't let me—the **busybody** is looking at my chats."

YEYÉ

In a nutshell: Remember the Valley girls? They were the rich California girls who had nothing better to do than paint their nails and say things like: "This is like, so awesome!". (They used the word *like* in every breath.) Their vanity knew no limits. Well, meet the **yeyés,** Panama's Valley girls—only it's a term that applies to both men and women alike. They are the yuppies, the up-and-coming, and the high class all in one. "Cuando llegas a un salón **yeyé,** crees que el tinte costará 100, y luego te dicen que son 300." Translation: "When you go to a *high class* beauty salon, you think to get your hair dyed it'll be 100 dollars, but then they tell you it's 300."

Another man posted: "Soy humildemente un raka disfraza'o de **yeyé.**" Translation: "I'm a just a humble commoner passing himself off as *high class.*"
As a group, they are known as **la yeyesada.** Panamanians say their affected speech sounds like people talking with potatoes in their mouths. They say **o sea** (that is) as frequently as the Valley girls said *like.* Like, gag me with a spoon, OK?

10

THE GOLDEN ÑAPA

¡LA BOTASTE!

Literal meaning: You threw it out!

In a nutshell: The game is tied with the bases loaded and you are up to bat. The crowd is going wild. The pitcher winds up, he throws, you swing and CLACK! It's going, going…GONE! **¡La botaste!** Yes, you hit it out of the park. So this means: *"You did a great job!"*.

With that same enthusiasm, dear reader, we congratulate you. You are now the proud owner of more than 200 key Panamanian words, phrases, and sayings. So keep listening. When you hear a new word or phrase, write it down. Find out what it means. And soon you will be more Panamanian than **guacho!** So put that **chonta** to work! **¡La botaste!**

*Forgot what a **ñapa** is? Go back to term #122.*

INDEX

A

abuelazón **38**
acholado **21**
A cualquiera se le muere un tío **105**
¿Adónde vai tú? **14**
agarrar los mangos bajitos **46**
a guanchinche **101**
ají chombo **22**
a la bulla de los cocos **110**
alborotar el congo **112**
alcahuete **113**
alelaò **142**
alelarse **142**
allá 'onde uno **14**
a lo mili **111**
amarrar la cara **143**
a monchinche **101**
andar con una pasta **144**
Ando arrastrando la manta **114**
añicos, Estoy hecho **114**
arranque **18**, **94**
arrepinchoso **144**

arroz con mango **113**
¡Aya la bestia! **15**
¡Aya la máquina! **15**
¡Aya la peste! **15**
¡Aya la vida! **15**

B

babieco **115**
baboso **70**
bagre **145**
bajareque **16**
balboa **19**
Barco parado no paga flete **115**
barriada bruja **118**
barriga pegada al espinazo, tener la **139**
bate **116**
batería **116**
Belén con los pastores, estar en **148**
bellaco **94**
bemba **136**
beri beri **80**

biberón **71**
bichareco **145**
biencuidaò **46**
biombo **16**
birrioso **146**
Bochinbook **117**
bochinche **117**
bola, en **9**
bollo, pelar el **73**
borriguero en mosaico enjabonado, Eres como **84**
borriguero por iguana, Vendían **84**
botaste!, ¡La **162**
bote, Dame un **17**
botella **47**
Bravos de Boston **48**
bruja, Me salió la **118**
buay **38**
buco **17, 35**
bulla de los cocos, a la **110**
bulto **47**
burundanga **60**

C

cabanga **131**
cacharpa **119**
cafá **120**
camarón **48, 89**
Camina como loro en cinc caliente **85**
campechano **147**
cara, amarrar la **143**
¡Carajo! **28**
carilimpio **121**
carimañola **60**
carretilla, hablar en **149**
carrizo **61**
carro de pifia **30**
cartucho **49**

casa bruja **118**
chaneado **95**
changa **61**
chantin **39**
chapa **49**
chapistero **49**
chécheres **18**
chen chen **19**
chévere **18**
chicha **9, 62**
chicha de guardia **62**
chicha de paipa **62**
chicha de piña **62**
chicha de policía **62**
chicheme **63**
chichi **39**
chichí **39**
chifear **121**
chin **20**
chingongo **63**
chinguear **50**
chino **64**
chiquillos **122**
chiquishow **122**
chirrisco **64**
chiva **85, 89**
chivo loco, hacerse el **149**
chiwis **65**
cholipay **21**
cholo **21**
Cholywood **21**
chomba **22**
chonta **79, 162**
chota **57**
chotear **96**
¡Chuleta! **23**
churrusco **79**
churuca **97**
churuquero **97**
clipsadora **50**

clipsar **50**

cobre, salírsele el **157**

cocobolo **78**

coger un cinco **24**

comearroz **43**

comer en paila **25**

comer pavo **156**

compa **99**

compinche **99**

concolón **66**

conflei **65**

congo, alborotar el **112**

congo, No seas **112**

cuara **19**

cucaracha en baile de gallinas, Me siento como **88**

cuero, Dale **36**

culantro, Está bueno el, pero no tanto **123**

culeco **40**

culecos, los **40**

culei, Eres como **98**

culiso **27**

D

daim **19**

Dale mili **111**

Dale p'alante! **30**

darle plomo **133**

darle rejera **41**

de Fidanque a Toledano **123**

de huevo a huevo **123**

destapar un tamal **122**

diablo rojo **26**

donde toca una lata **98**

E

el hijo de Lindbergh **150**

El que mucho abarca, poco aprieta **11**

embellacarse **94**

engoma'o **128**

Eres como borriguero en mosaico enjabonado **84**

Eres como culei **98**

Es bueno el culantro, pero no tanto **123**

estar como gorgojos **125**

estar en Belén con los pastores **148**

estar en las nebulosas **148**

estar en panga **140**

Estoy en la cama de los perros **120**

Estoy hecho añicos **114**

Estoy limpio **120**

Estoy pela'o **120**

F

faracho **80**

Fidanque **123**

Fidel Castro **23**

firi firi **80**

flete, Barco parado no paga **115**

fren **99, 103**

fulano **145**

fulo **10, 27**

fulo, Salió el **27**

G

gallada **86**

gallina del patio **76**

gallinero **86**

gallo **86**

golpe de ala **81**

gorgojos, estar como **125**

grajiento **81**

grajo **81**

gringo **22**

guacha, hasta la **126**

165

guachimán **51**
guacho **67**, **162**
guapachoso **147**
guarapo **68**
guaro **64**
guial **41**
guichi guaiper **51**

H

hablar en carretilla **149**
hacer patacón **72**
hacerse el chivo loco **149**
hacer una vaca **100**
hasta la guacha **126**
hielo seco **52**
hombro, manga por **129**
huesear **53**

I

inchipinchi **42**, **99**, **103**
interioranos **14**

J

¡Jo! **28**
jorón **68**
Jugué muerto **127**
Jugué vivo **127**
juma'o **128**

L

¡La botaste! **162**
levante **42**
limpio, Estoy **120**
Lindbergh, más perdido que el hijo de **150**
lista chomba **22**

llovizna **16**
Lo que 'tá para el perro no se lo come el micho **87**
loro en cinc caliente, Camina como **85**
Loro viejo no da pata **128**
luz bruja **118**

M

mafá **69**
mamadera **71**
man **28**
mangalarga **73**
manga por hombro **129**
mango, arroz con **113**
mangos bajitos, agarrar los **46**
manso **29**
manta, Ando arrastrando la **114**
manzanillo **130**
Martín Moreno, que quita lo malo y pone lo bueno **41**
más perdido que el hijo de Lindbergh **150**
Me salió la bruja **118**
Me siento como cucaracha en baile de gallinas **88**
¡Meto! **29**
metrobuses **26**
micho **87**
mili, a lo **111**
mili, Dale **111**
mococoa **131**
mola **53**
moñon **82**
monta'o **54**
mosca, Ponte **90**
motor de arranque **94**
muerto, Jugué **127**
mula **89**

murga **107**

N

ñame baboso **70**
ñampeaó **70**
ñáñara **131**
ñapa **101**, **162**
neveras **26**
No seas congo **112**
No tengo ni un rial **120**
No tengo pepita en la lengua **151**

P

paganini **152**
paila, comer en **25**
palancas **26**
p'alante **30**
panga, estar en **140**
parkin **102**
parquear **102**
pasiero **42**, **99**, **103**
pasta, andar con una **144**
pataconcito **132**
patacones **72**, **132**
patacón, hacer **72**
pata, Loro viejo no da **128**
patatú **80**
pavearse **90**
paviolo **90**
pavo **26**
pavo, comer **156**
pay **103**
pecueca **82**
pegaó **72**
pela'ito **43**
pelaó **23**
pelar el bollo **73**
pelo cholo **21**
pepita en la lengua, No tengo **151**

perdida **150**
perro no se lo come el micho, Lo que 'tá para el **87**
perros, Estoy en la cama de los **120**
perro tinaquero **91**
pescuezona **73**
pezuña **101**
picado **153**
pichicuma **153**
piedrero **132**
pifia **30**
pilinqui **153**
pillar **31**
pinta **73**
pipa **74**
pipón **74**
piquera **54**, **102**
piquete **32**
pitufo **57**
plena **104**
plomo **133**
plomo, darle **133**
pocotón **17**
policía muerto **57**
ponchera **33**
ponerse el carro de sombrero **134**
¡Ponte mosca! **90**
porcon **75**
priti **104**
pulpear **55**
Puro tilín, tilín, y nada de paleta **124**
push **135**
push button **135**

Q

¿Qué e' lo que e'? **34**
queloqué **34**
quemacoco **78**

¡Qué piquete! **32**
¡Qué priti! **104**
¿Qué xopá? **34**
quitafrío **42**

R

racataca **154**
radio bemba **136**
rambulería **137**
rantan **17**, **35**
rayarse **155**
rejera, darle **41**
repelón **137**
revosh **56**
rial, No tengo ni un **120**
riveteaʾo **95**
rompepecho **73**
ropa vieja **75**
rosca **138**
rumbero **156**
runcho **139**

S

Sabe más que tío Conejo **158**
salírsele el cobre **157**
saloma **56**
saltar garrocha **76**
sancocho **76**
sapear **92**
sarao **105**
Sarna con gusto no pica **106**
sombrero, ponerse el carro de **134**

T

tallaʾo **95**

tamal, destapar un **122**
tarrantan **35**
tatái **35**
tener la barriga pegada al espinazo **139**
tilín, tilín, y nada de paleta, Puro **124**
tinaco **91**
tío, A cualquiera se le muere un **105**
tío Conejo, Sabe más que **158**
tiro al concolón **66**
tongo **57**
tranque **29**, **58**
transar **138**
trinche **97**
truñuño **153**
tuna **107**

V

vaca, hacer una **100**
Vendían borriguero por iguana **84**
vidajena **159**
violinista **108**
vivo, Jugué **127**

Y

yeyé **160**
yeyesada **160**

Z

zambito **44**
zurrarse **58**
zurra zurra **58**

COSTA RICAN
SPANISH
SPEAK LIKE A NATIVE!

LEE JAMISON

GUATEMALAN
SPANISH
SPEAK LIKE A NATIVE!

LEE JAMISON

**BURNING
TONGUE**
MEXICAN SPANISH

LEE JAMISON

Become an
ins**i**der
What are you waiting for?

NICARAGUAN
SPANISH
SPEAK LIKE A NATIVE!

LEE JAMISON

PANAMANIAN
SPANISH
SPEAK LIKE A NATIVE!

LEE JAMISON

PHOTO CREDITS

Cover: Balboa coin, © info78469/bigstock.com; Ship, © dani3315/bigstock.com; Old lady, Roman Königshofer | Filmmaker & Photographer via Foter.com / CC BY-ND; Pollera girl, Ayaita via Foter.com / CC BY-SA; Toucan portrait closeup, © amenpercy - Fotolia; Arriving at a Caribbean tropical Island, San Blas, Panama. Traveling Central America, © diegocardini - fotolia.com; Large cruise ship entering Panama City, © dani3315 - fotolia.com; Panamanian figurines, © Lee Jamison; **Page 13:** couple of dogs on the phone, © javier brosch/bigstock.com; **Page 15:** Surprised woman, © Kurhan - fotolia.com; **Page 16:** slingshot, © Photo Sunday/bigstock.com; **Page 17:** Surprised woman, © Kurhan/bigstock.com **Page 19:** United States Quarter Dollar Obverse, © United States Mint; **Page 20:** Chinese woman, © hanack - fotolia.com; **Page 21:** Popcorn, © urfingus/bigstock.com; **Page 23:** Fresh Bone-In Pork Chop Isolated Over White, © Bill - fotolia.com; **Page 24:** Newborn Baby Boy Sleeping in a Rustic Crate, © katrinaelena - fotolia.com; **Page 26:** Turkey, © fotomaster - fotolia.com; **Page 30:** sexy legs, black heels, © Klemen Petrič - fotolia.com; **Page 33:** White wine up to red wine, © misaleva - fotolia.com; **Page 37:** dad mum and son sizes shoes in family love concept, © Focus Pocus LTD - fotolia.com; **Page 39:** Pink pacifier, © Coprid/bigstock .com; **Page 40:** live chicken bird redhead looks at three eggs isolated on white, © maxim ibragimov/bigstock.com; **Page 41:** Leather belt, © Alexey Lobur/bigstock.com; **Page 43:** Rice in a bowl, © sommai/bigstock.com; **Page 44:** Young girl, © Kamira/bigstock.com; **Page 45:** San Blas, Kuna Yala, Panama, © benkucinski / photo on flickr; **Page 46:** Mangos, © linda_vostrovska - fotolia.com; **Page 47:** Cardboard box, © Scanrail/bigstock.com; **Page 48:** shrimp, © Kittisak Jirasittichai/bigstock.com; **Page 49:** Plastic Grocery Bag / with clipping path, © sumire8 - fotolia.com; **Page 50:** Blue office stapler, © modustollens/bigstock.com; **Page 52:** styrofoam sheets, © olgavolodina/ bigstock.com; **Page 55:** Beautiful business woman with six arms, © llhedgehogll - fotolia.com; **Page 57:** Police Car Top View Isolated, © Tomasz Zajda - fotolia.com; **Page 59:** Food for thought, © Tijana - fotolia.com; **Page 61:** Drinking straw, © Jamroen Jaiman/bigstock.com; **Page 63:** Chewing gum plate wrapped in red foil, © UserSam2007/bigstock.com; **Page 65:** cereal, © Seregam/bigstock.com; **Page 69:** Fried Braided Bread, © cratervalley - fotolia.com; **Page 71:** Baby bottle vector, © andegro4ka/bigstock.com; **Page 72:** tostones, fried green plantain banana chips, © oysy/bigstock.com; **Page 74:** Broken raw ripe coconut, © Pavlo Kucherov/bigstock.com; **Page 76:** Stabhochsprung Vektor, © Silveryil - fotolia.com; **Page 77:** Man sees other self in mirror, © rolffimages/bigstock .com; **Page 78:** Coconut on beach, © Rqs/bigstock.com; **Page 82:** Black hair isolated, © Elena Kharichkina - fotolia.com; **Page 83:** Red kitten, © Alena Ozerova - fotolia.com; **Page 84:** gray lizard, © balakleypb - fotolia.com; **Page 86:** Rooster, © Anan Kaewkhammul/bigstock.com; **Page 87:** Cat headphones, © Rasulov/bigstock.com; **Page 88:** Dancing GMO chicken seated in a oven, © smithore/bigstock.com; **Page 89:** Silhouette of a donkey, © tcheres - fotolia.com; Silhouettes of trucks on a white background. Vector, © norsob - fotolia.com; **Page 91:** Trash dog, © danilobiancalana - fotolia.com; **Page 92:** Toad, © kareinick/bigstock.com; **Page 93:** Smiling boy gives thumbs up sign, cantor pannatto - fotolia.com, © rubberball - fotolia.com; **Page 95:** Red high heels, © Elnur/bigstock.com; **Page 96:** French bulldog giving high five with female hand over black, © Patryk Kosmider/bigstock.com; **Page 99:** Group of friends having fun, © oneinchpunch - fotolia.com; **Page 100:** Piggy bank, © Joop Hoek - fotolia.com; **Page 107:** tuna, © AlenVL/bigstock.com; trumpet, © Kayco/bigstock.com; **Page 108:** Violin, © makou - fotolia .com; **Page 109:** Undercover hooded stranger in the dark, © ra2 studio - fotolia.com; **Page 110:** Coconut in water splash isolated on white, © aragami12345/bigstock.com; **Page 112:** Illustration of angry bee mascot, © Tigateluloro/bigstock.com; **Page 114:** Sad Teddy, © Phils Photography - fotolia.com; **Page 116:** Cheat sheet, © Yastremska/ bigstock.com; **Page 117:** Whispering secrets, © olly - fotolia.com; **Page 118:** Financial projections, © cartoonresource - fotolia.com; **Page 123:** Fresh culantro,Sawtooth Coriander - Eryngium foetidum, © daguwan - fotolia .com; **Page 124:** Old bell isolated on white background, © kuarmungadd - fotolia.com; **Page 125:** close up of weevil destroy rice, © krsprs - fotolia.com; **Page 126:** bolts and nut on wood background, © Kittiphat/bigstock.com; **Page 129:** Large leather sofa with a bunch of different things, © Zarya Maxim - fotolia.com; **Page 131:** small man resting on the big head man, © ArtFamily - fotolia.com; **Page 133:** Bullet isolated on white background, © yingthun - fotolia.com; **Page 134:** Car crash, detail, © Alexey Zarodov - fotolia.com; **Page 135:** Red button, © montego6 - fotolia.com; **Page 136:** Radio, © blueringmedia - fotolia.com; Isolated red lips, © tverdohlib - fotolia .com; **Page 140:** Bicycle toy on white backgound, © Phawat khommai - fotolia.com; **Page 141:** A colourful head, © olly - fotolia.com; **Page 143:** man and woman changed faces, © ArtFamily - fotolia.com; **Page 145:** catfish, © 7activestudio - fotolia.com; **Page 146:** Group of cartoon sport fans and supporters cheering, © denis_pc - fotolia .com; **Page 150:** Smartphone with missed call notification on screen, © viperagp - fotolia.com; **Page 151:** Girl making jokes, © olly - fotolia.com; **Page 155:** Crazy woman using smartphone and yelling over blackboard, © vadymvdrobot - fotolia.com; **Page 156:** Turkey dancing, © corythoman - fotolia.com; **Page 157:** Angry elderly man, © olly - fotolia.com; **Page 158:** Cartoon rabbit reading a book, © sarah5 - fotolia.com; **Page 159:** Wow notebook, © Antonio Gravante - fotolia.com; **Page 161:** Gold egg, © HP_Photo - fotolia.com; **Page 162:** Baseball, Sport, Baseballs, © BillionPhotos.com - fotolia.com; **Page 170:** Old reflex camera, © paweorowski - Fotolia

Made in the USA
Middletown, DE
30 April 2023

29770809R00097